The Scuppernong Press: www.thescuppernongpress.com

First trade paperback edition
Manufactured in the United States of America

Library of Congress Control Number: 2006925175

International Standard Book Number (ISBN) 0-9773156-5-7

The Day the
Black Rain
Fell

W. F. Shelton

Introduction by
James S. Warren

The Scuppernong Press
Wake Forest, NC

The Coley brothers at the end

The Last Legal Hanging in Franklin County
(The Day the Black Rain Fell)

The young-uns rode the wagons in their Sunday clothes
People came from all directions up them red dirt roads
They was headed to the jailhouse in the dog day sun
To gather round the gallows and see justice done
Singing shall we gather at the river?
The beautiful, beautiful river?
They sang shall we gather at the river
As they rumbled toward the jail
On the day the Black Rain fell

It was Tom and Calvin Coley they had come to see
Two highway robbin' brothers from another county
They'd flagged a traveling peddler down one night in the rain
And then they beat him to death
For a handful of change
And it was shall we gather at the river
The beautiful, beautiful river?
They heard shall we gather at the river
As they waited in that cell
On the Day the Black Rain fell

Tom said to Calvin, I think I'm feeling sick
Whatever they're gonna do, I hope they do it quick
Calvin said to Tom you know I understand
But you need to choke it down and try to die like a man
And it was shall we gather at the river
The beautiful, beautiful river
It was shall we gather at the river
They could hear an old church bell
On the day the Black Rain Fell

They could see some clouds had gathered as they stepped outside
On that short walk to the gallows and the other side
Right then a shadow passed over the crowd I'm told
And the sky grew strangely dark and the air got cold
And it was shall we gather at the river
The beautiful, beautiful river
The crowd sang shall we gather at the river
Like a false-hearted farewell
On the day the Black Rain Fell

It was over in a little while the deed was done
The people slowly turned to make their way back home
But not before the thunder sounded overhead
And the streets filled up with water like a riverbed

The rain was black as coal and had a sulfur smell
That hung around for days outside the county jail
The people were convinced it was the devil's rain
Cause the clothes they wore that day
They never would come clean

Shall we gather at the river
The beautiful, beautiful river?
When I hear shall we gather at the river
I still think about that tale
Of the day the Black Rain fell.

—lyrics by Thomas Scott Pearce ©2005

For Anne Freeman Shelton

… beloved wife, mother and grandmother

Introduction

Booze. A ghastly murder. Robbery. Daylight jailbreak. Adulterous prosecution witnesses. Jury nullification. Media circus. Hints of racism. Hired "legal" guns to prop up a faltering prosecution. Sound like one of our modern-day, made-for-cable trials? Not quite.

Against the backdrop of thousands of gawking and disorderly onlookers, a Franklin County Sheriff, oversees the public hanging of the Coley brothers for the murder of a Jewish peddler. On a stormy July afternoon, Friday the 13th 1894, Tom and Calvin Coley meet death at the end of a rope in the shadow of the Franklin County Courthouse in Louisburg, North Carolina. Later they were carried by wagon through a little hamlet called Wood to be buried in Nash County where they were born.

Originally published in 1984 by the late W. F. Shelton, *The Day the Black Rain Fell* is part whodunit, part courtroom drama and a vivid re-telling of crime and punishment a hundred or so years ago. Shelton, a former mayor, Recorder's Court judge, theater operator and accountant, brings to life that balmy day when honorable men, obligated to uphold the "rule of law," mete out a horrific punishment.

Hangings were carried out on the county level to show the citizenry what could happen to one who ran afoul of the law. It was thought that public hangings would be a deterrent to crime. Maybe they were, but they were also a great spectacle for the community whenever they occurred. In the 1890's approximately 1,000 people lived in Louisburg, yet 10,000 people turned out on judgment day for the Coley brothers' execution. After all, this was a double hanging—a first for Franklin County.

Despite the sheriff's disgust at the convergence of thousands on the tiny town as if they were attending the circus or county fair, he calmly proceeds with the last minute details of the execution. Threatening thunderstorms build in the distance; the sheriff orders the traps sprung. The heavens unleash a torrent of black rain on the dangling and dying brothers—and those who put them to death—forever stamping that infamous Friday the 13th into the memories and consciousness of the citizenry of Franklin County and the entire state of North Carolina.

Shelton imagines for us a time when average folks—fathers, husbands, working men and tobacco farmers—were forced to weigh the consequences of "clean" hangings versus "unclean" hangings. He describes a town's leadership obligated by law to decide how much money was enough money to spend on a gallows in order to provide a humane execution to exact punishment for an inhumane crime. Shelton questions whether the hurriedly built gallows containing only eleven steps rather than the customary, if somewhat superstitious thirteen, may have cheated a man out of a painless death. A callous observer on that dark day might have asked, "Why did it matter? An evil-doer was getting his just reward."

Yet, Shelton does more than re-tell a trial and a botched execution. He re-creates the story of *that* other humid day, nearly two years earlier. A day like any other in the young life of Samuel Tucker, a traveling salesman, who met his fate in a shanty occupied by two prostitutes and their boyfriends on the outskirts of Franklin County's Gold Mine Township. Some years before that fateful evening, the young man, a Russian Jew, had immigrated to America, seeking freedom from Czarist oppression and a chance to fulfill that basic of human desires—work. He was a living example of the "American Dream."

Samuel sold goods and wares door-to-door to folks living in the backwoods. Trusting and affable, his customers often offered him a meal and a bed that he would graciously accept. Unfortunately on July 30, 1892, he broke bread with the wrong sort. Before the end of the evening Samuel would be murdered for the hard-earned money in his pocket and robbed of all of his earthly possessions. If that wasn't indignity enough, the naïve salesman was thrown into a gully where his body lay for more than a year. With no family or friends to report him missing, Samuel's disappearance went unnoticed while his murderers enjoyed the fruits of their crime and continued along their merry way.

Yet, as numerous criminals can attest—nobody gets away with murder.

Though it was a different era—no telephones, no electricity, no automobiles—word spread quickly as the media sensationalized the murder and the trial. The Franklin County Sheriff lived in Franklinton where each morning he boarded the train to go to work in Louisburg. The county could afford but one deputy. Still, even with these constraints, the wheels of justice moved quickly a century ago. The Coleys' murder trial started less than a month after their arrest. The trial lasted three days, one day to select a jury, one day for the trial and one day for the jury to deliberate. Hardly two months passed before they were sentenced to hang.

Flawlessly, Shelton reconstructs the court procedures of 1894. While it may take more time for criminals to pass through today's legal system, those procedures have changed very little. *The Day the Black Rain Fell* is illustrative of how stable our justice system is in regard to trying criminals. The defendants were well represented by attorneys assigned to them by the state. As is often the case today, the most significant decision a defense attorney will make is whether to allow a defendant to testify. Judge John Bynum, from Greensboro, was extremely careful not to speak to anyone about the case and continually admonished the jury to do likewise. The verdict of the jury and the decisions of the judge would be made strictly upon evidence presented in the courtroom, not from what they heard or read elsewhere.

Prior to the brothers' arrest there was only the criminal charge of murder, no second degree or manslaughter existed; however the legislature had changed the law between Samuel's murder and the Coleys' trial. Thus, the defense saw an opening for the Supreme Court to overturn the case and immediately appealed their clients' guilty verdict. Compared to present death penalty cases, the Court acted with lightning speed, swiftly and decisively upholding the jury's decision.

The transcript of the trial taken by the court reporter well documented all the evidence presented and can be found in our North Carolina state archives, Volume 114 of the *North Carolina Reports.*

What is the mystery of the rumored black rain that fell that July day? Was it more than just rain falling through dust drummed by throngs of curious onlookers? Or was it something more metaphysical? Is the Black Rain a metaphor for a kind of stain on Franklin County's history because proper heed was not taken to pay and build a proper gallows? A symbol of an "unclean" hanging, perhaps?

Regardless of what really happened that Friday the 13th, no one can dispute the fact that Franklin County's citizens and many people from across the state bore final witness to a barbaric punishment. The Coleys' deaths ultimately lead to the demise of county seat hangings.

So read on. Shelton's account intrigues, informs, and yes, *The Day the Black Rain Fell* holds your attention to the very end.

— *James S. Warren*
Wake Forest, North Carolina
2006

The Day the Black Rain Fell

The Day the
Black Rain
Fell

W. F. Shelton

The Day the Black Rain Fell

Chapter 1

Sheriff Henry Crawford Kearney of Franklinton was serving one of his several terms as the Sheriff of Franklin County. As is often the case, he had been opposed in many of his several elections, then, and in terms of office that followed the happenings discussed here. Possibly his fine record as a lieutenant in General Robert E. Lee's Army of Northern Virginia had helped ensure his elections. Also, Sheriff Kearney had undoubtedly been active in the quiet but determined efforts of our citizens to free themselves and the ruling of North Carolina from the carpetbaggers and their cohorts. Sheriff Kearney was the bearer of a nickname, "Big Henry." The nickname was to distinguish him from a distant cousin bearing the same name, H.C. Kearney, who, in addition to being much smaller than the Sheriff, was a law officer; Constable Kearney was, of course, "Little Henry." When Lee's surrender at Appomattox took place, Sheriff Kearney had personally signed the "paroles" of his men as they were discharged under the orders of Union officers. With his duty done, he returned to his home in Franklinton.

The sheriff had had to participate in single hangings several times in his career. But, this particular hanging in July of 1894 was his first "double." The county commissioners had appropriated seventy-five dollars to build the double scaffold. Buck Johnson had been hired to build the simple structure, which had a framework of six, four-by-six timbers which Johnson had specially cut at a local sawmill. The timbers were sixteen feet long and were mounted, three upright on the front, with the horizontal crosspiece over these uprights. This crosspiece would take the two ropes. A platform, reached by eleven steps—not the traditional thirteen—was some six feet above the ground. The platform had room for eight chairs for the doctors, the ministers and the official witnesses. The front part of the platform was taken up by the two falling traps. These traps were hinged at the rear by large metal barn door hinges, while the front of the traps were held in place by a slanted four-by-four timber. The mechanism was simple. The four-by-fours were just knocked aside by the executioners and the traps, supposedly then bearing their burdens, would immediately fall. It was simple, inexpensive and practically guaranteed to send the trap's occupants on their final trip. The Franklin County Commissioners were apparently in a savings mood when the gallows cost upward of three hundred dollars or more. Other counties had spent that much.

Hanging was by law "public" so that salutary effects of encouraging law-abiding citizens to remain that way could have full sway. These county-seat executions were always well attended by the public. But such attendance, it seems now, was more out of morbid curiosity than to absorb the good effects that might come out of such displays. The public had further turned these hangings into carnivals. Often there would be souvenir stands and small bazaars opened by enterprising citizens to take full advantage of the large crowds that gathered for these events. A double hanging, the sheriff feared, would bring more people to

Louisburg than had ever been assembled in that town of one thousand souls. This large crowd was anticipated by the sheriff even before the two doomed men had made their widely publicized escape. The trial of the two young men and their escape had received thorough coverage from the *Raleigh News and Observer* and had been printed throughout the South by the organization that later became the Associated Press. The conviction of the Coley Boys and their later sentence to be hanged had received front-page coverage in Raleigh, and other newspapers. The Raleigh paper even printed woodcut drawings of the two men along with stories of the trial.

Sheriff Kearney was an early "commuter" in that, he came to work on Mondays on the ten-mile track of the Louisburg Railway, which opened its spur line to the Raleigh and Gaston Railroad at Franklinton about 1885. There was a turntable at Franklinton, and the one locomotive owned by the Louisburg line was thus turned for the two round trips that the railway made to Franklinton each day. The Louisburg Railway was later to become part of the Raleigh and Gaston line, which eventually joined the Seaboard Air Line Railway. Sheriff Kearney had a room in Louisburg and on either Friday afternoon or Saturday, depending on the work at hand, returned to his family in Franklinton. The sheriff kept a mare and buggy in Louisburg for him and his deputies to use in serving in law enforcement and process serving.

There was only one deputy, Norman Stokes, who assisted in law enforcement and the service of court papers. Kearney's office was just to the right past the main entrance of the box-like brick square that served as the Franklin County Courthouse. The entire second floor of the courthouse had the courtroom and such anterooms as required for the judge's chambers and a jury room. Other county offices occupied the rest of the first floor of the building. The sanitary facilities in those days before sewage was served by segregated brick privies at the rear of the building.

As the sheriff inspected the double gallows built on the right side of the Franklin County jail, some eight hundred feet to the east of the courthouse, he thought of his most unpleasant job in being sheriff, that of being the executioner at hangings. In his Civil War experience the sheriff had seen death on the battlefields, but death in battle was not the same thing as the deliberate ending of a human life.

A hanging was certainly not a pretty thing to watch as the body did a vast amount of trembling and sphincters that controlled body wastes were loosed for their final release of these wastes. This was the result of a "clean" hanging. But, as sometimes happened, the noose knot slipped either to the front or the rear of the neck and the neck was not broken in the fall. If that happened, one had to wait while the unfortunate subject gyrated in the air and slowly choked to death. This was the unclean hanging. The clean hanging was supposedly painless when the knot was in the proper place. While the use of black hoods for the victims was standard at some executions, they were not used in county-seat hangings. So, it follows that the unclean hangings would fully expose the expression and the fruitless writhing as the body sought in vain for the air to sustain life. And this must be borne out by the executioners, since once the traps had fallen, there was no going back to properly adjust the noose.

Sheriff Kearney wished that his two prisoners would go the quick, painless way. He wished that the knot would stay in place under the ear of each of the men during their six-foot drop. Another wish of the sheriff's was that the mob of avidly curious people would stay at home on the fateful day. He much preferred that the march from the jail to the gallows, and the subsequent removal of bodies, be done only in the presence of the official witnesses. He wished mightily that the public would not make a spectacle of the double execution. But, being a realist, he also felt that his wishes in this respect would not be granted. And, he was right.

Sheriff Kearney had written out the names of the official witnesses to the execution. He knew them all by heart now. Two ministers, two doctors and four other citizens that he had selected from the County Board of Commissioners and from the public. Not only would the official witnesses see the hanging, but the great publicity that the case had received would attract many thousands of unofficial witnesses.

Once more the sheriff inspected his carpenter's handiwork and tested the two simple timbers what would release the trap. The traps would hold, he thought, and release their burdens properly. One of the fifteen-foot long sections of rope was hanging in Jailer Pinnell's little alcove of an office. The second rope would be brought later by the Wake County Sheriff. This second rope, the sheriff had been told, had a long and gruesome history.

Captain S.S. Meadows, Commander of the Franklin Guards, drove up in his buggy when the sheriff came down from the platform. The sheriff talked briefly with Meadows and told him that there was nothing new from Gold Mine Township on the often-rumored delivery of his guests. If any of the prisoners' drinking buddies were going to make a jail break to free the Coleys, it had better be soon. Captain Meadows spoke to Corporal Mortimer Pleasants, who was in charge of the five privates then on guard about the jail yard. The Franklin Guard had been posted at the jail since late in June when the two prisoners had actually escaped from their cells. There were also rumors that reached the sheriff that there would be some attempt by the Coley Boys' friends to free the two men. Kearney had called in Captain Meadows and the blue-coated guards rather than take chances. The sheriff could stand the sight of the blue-coated guards around his jail much better than he could stand losing his prisoners. Besides, these blue coats, an anathema during his Civil War Service, were worn by Southern boys now.

The day of the black rain was at hand.

Chapter II

S amuel Tucker, recently an immigrant from Russia, was twenty-five years of age. His youth served him well in trudging the dusty clay roads of rural Franklin County with his hand-piled cart. In spite of his youth, the young man was tired on that Thursday, July 30, 1892. He had been on the road since sun-up and although his cart was much lighter than it had been a few days before, the cart was a burden. Once Tucker had made up his mind to quit selling for the day, he headed down the next set of wagon tracks in Gold Mine Township to seek lodging for the night. He reflected how Gold Mine had received its name since he had recently passed the great red hills of the Portis Gold Mine, now idled since the slaves were gone. Tucker recalled that it was a Jewish peddler, such as himself, who helped turn Isaac Portis from a hardscrabble farmer into a wealthy gold miner. Like Tucker was accustomed to doing, this earlier peddler had told Portis that the glittering particles in the mud chinking of the cabin were possibly gold. Portis thanked his overnight guest and sent off samples of his soil to Richmond for assay. The farmer stopped tilling his soil soon thereafter, and in the twenty-five years prior to 1855, Portis and some of his neighbors had shipped more than three million dollars in gold to the Richmond Mint. That Jewish peddler had brought wealth to someone other than himself. In 1855 this all ended when rich lodes were discovered at Sutter's Mill in California.

Tucker thought of his coming to America those few

years back to escape the pogroms that were persecuting his people in Czarist Russia. He grinned wryly at the remembrance of his trips to Richmond and to Raleigh to refill his cart. The trips always ended in hand-waving arguments and bargaining over prices his suppliers charged. But often, after these heated buying sessions were over, the young peddler would be asked to dinner, the highly excited arguing over prices completely forgotten. Tucker preferred buying in Richmond since he could go to the Synagogue there. He had joined the Jewish congregation there soon after arriving in this country. The peddler thought of his next buying trip since his stock was getting picked over. He fondled the one hundred and sixty-nine dollars in his coat, now resting on the cart since the day was hot. The money was beside a small caliber revolver. Robbery of such merchants was not unknown by the many immigrant Jews who had taken up his profession of peddling cloth and household supplies from a pushcart. Some of these immigrant young men had already collected a sufficient stake to open a permanent store. Such a store was the desire of Samuel Tucker. He promised himself that he would be often in the Temple, once he had his store in operation.

Tucker pulled his mind back to his present state. He needed rest, food and a bath. His first stop was at the home of N. C. Gupton, but his farmer had several children and did not have room for a guest. However, the farmer did direct Tucker to a small house he would find some eight hundred yards down the road, where two women named Lucy and Pinkey had recently moved. The peddler thanked

Gupton and started to move on, but Gupton called him back to discharge his duty that he, as a Christian, church-going man, felt was his. He told Tucker that the house at the end of the wagon track had been earning a bad reputation and often drunken parties and strange men passed up and down the lane, frequently after dark. Apparently the two women and their two dark-haired boyfriends, Thomas and Calvin Coley, had been either bootlegging or conducting other business from the house. Even so, the peddler was tired and felt that he could tend to his own business when expedient to do so. He would welcome a chance to rest, even in the house with a poor reputation and, besides, Gupton was probably exaggerating.

Gupton was not exaggerating. Already he and several of his neighbors had been discussing ways and means of getting the two women to move on. The sounds of ribald revelry had more than once awakened the farmer and his wife. Gupton intended to bring the situation to the attention of Sheriff Kearney the next time he was in Louisburg.

Lucy Brewer smiled at most men. She smiled at Samuel Tucker as she agreed to let the peddler have supper and spend the night. She showed Tucker to a single bed in a small room off a passage between the room and the house. A few minutes later, he went to the other part of the house and was introduced to Pinkey Wilkins, whom Lucy called her sister, and to Calvin Coley, a tall, sharp-eyed young man with curly black hair and a drooping moustache. Tucker estimated that Calvin, whom the women addressed as "Cal," was about his own age, but considerably heavier. A bit later, when a supper of cabbage and some kind of dark meat was served, Thomas Coley arrived and was introduced to the peddler. Tom appeared about five years his brother's elder and had a moustache and black hair to match Cal's. Tom had little to say and it was soon apparent to Tucker that Calvin apparently had most of the brains of the Coley boys since he did most of the talking, as if Tom were not quite bright. That Cal did the thinking for the two brothers was being constantly borne out by Tom's nodding his head and in almost constant assent to what Cal was saying. Cal talked on this subject and that subject, but the peddler had nothing to say except an occasional assent to Cal's talk. The peddler noted with some concern that Cal and Tom took long pulls from a stone jug set in the middle of the table. The odor of the potent whiskey in the jug filled the room. At the completion of the meal, Cal and Tom went into the corner of the kitchen and had a whispered conference, well out of earshot of the women and the peddler. Tucker noted that Cal was doing most of the talking in the conference and, as usual, Tom was nodding his head in silent agreement with what Cal was saying.

After supper, the five took chairs from the kitchen and moved out under the shade of an old oak in the yard. Tucker noticed that Tom was watching him closely, although the elder Coley tried not to let Tucker see his sidelong glances. As the sun was preparing to set, Cal, at a suggestion from Lucy, went into the house and returned with the liquor jug and a battered five-string banjo. Cal was the musician and gave his own rendition of several Civil War songs. Frequent recourse to the stone jug by Cal and Tom soon had Cal hitting false notes and forgetting parts of the songs he was singing. Soon the singing stopped and Cal and Tom told about their father, Sam, whom they said was a great expert on the fiddle, as well as the banjo.

The gaiety of such an evening was strangely missing. As the brothers continued their tippling from the jug, it seemed apparent to Tucker that he was getting outright hostile stares from the two dark-haired men. The women were strangely silent. As the sun was nearing setting, Tucker bade the others goodnight and carried his chair back into the kitchen. Tucker was uneasily thinking of the apparent hostile stares that the brothers had been giving him. So the peddler got a bucket of water from the outdoor well, back of the kitchen, and went into his small room as the light began to fail. Here, he took his bath as the murmuring and a few notes from the banjo came from outside. The room was stifling hot in spite of an open window over the bed. What breeze that had been found under the oak failed to reach this part of the house. Tucker tried to sleep but when that proved impossible, he took the one chair in the room out to a passage and sat waiting for the air to cool. He had undressed and donned his nightclothes after taking his bath out of the bucket. The money and gun were left in the room with his clothes.

Perhaps it was the uneasiness of his surroundings that kept the peddler awake; perhaps the heat. The muffled talking out under the oak continued with the voice of

Calvin, and occasionally, the voice of Tom, becoming more and more slurred under the influence of the whiskey. Tucker remembered, with increasing worry, the unsmiling stares of the two men. He recalled with alarm the many robberies of such peddlers as himself—and the murders, also—of several of his fellows. He noted that the sound from the oak tree had ceased, and he arose to check the small pistol in his coat pocket. He made a mental note to remember exactly where the coat and pistol were located. The sun had long since set and bright moon was now controlling the sky. A small breeze had arisen in the hallway, making his seat there more comfortable than his room. All sound had ceased from the other occupants in the house and the night was still except for a chorus of crickets.

"Ain't you a sonofabitch that called me a kinky-headed nigger?"

"I haven't called you anything," Tucker gasped.

Tucker arose in panic, but both hands of Calvin Coley now gripped the peddler's throat. The young Jew tried to struggle free and tried also to get to his room for the gun, just a few feet away. Tucker's struggles and his words of denial were loosening Cal's grip on his throat and the peddler might have gotten away from his assailant had not Tom Coley entered the scene from behind the young Jew. Tom grasped a bear hug around the peddler, pinning the arms and pulling that young man into the yard, near a chopping block. Tom threw the struggling man to the ground. Tucker started to rise so he failed to see when Cal struck the first blow with an axe to the peddler's head. Lucy and Pinkey arrived at the scene to dimly see a second blow struck by Cal. The two women shuddered in horror as the young Jew died after a few minutes of aimless kicking at the dust. Lucy thought of the wild thrashing of a chicken whose neck had just been wrung. She suddenly realized that this very thing she had witnessed had been planned during the whispered conference between the brothers at suppertime. The two women, after being ordered by Cal to help, assisted in stripping the nightclothes from the slight body. They were also ordered by Cal to assist in carrying the body. A lantern was produced and a macabre procession started for a dense honeysuckle ravine some five hundred yards from the house. Tom, Lucy, and Pinkey took the other limbs of the inert form. The body was rolled into the ravine. At the bottom of the ravine, the body came to rest, face up to the stars with unseeing eyes. The two brothers soon covered the evidence of their crime with leaves, pine branches and vines.

Back at the house, the four set about dividing up the loot. The brothers took the small amount of men's clothing from the cart. The women took the dress goods and trinkets. Cal pocketed the gun, and the money was divided among the four. The peddler's bloody nightclothes were burned in the kitchen stove. The empty cart was stored in an outbuilding at the house.

The body of Samuel Tucker was to rest, undisturbed except for the ravages of time and nature a full eighteen months. For as summer held its grip on Franklin County and the rains came to give growth to the honeysuckle, the vines grew lushly in the ravine to cover the thing that greed had done.

Chapter III

The murder had occurred on Thursday night, The following Saturday saw the Coley's and their mistresses take the Louisburg train to Franklinton, then by train to Raleigh and thence to Durham. Later the four went on to Norfolk. The house in Gold Mine Township stood empty for eight weeks. Then, just as quietly as they had left, Tom and Lucy returned to the house, their shares from the murder gone. Tom worked in the sawmills or in the tobacco fields of the area. Employers of Tom said he "wasn't strong in the head" but he could handle a cant hook at the local sawmills and could pull tobacco with the best of them. But, Tom was a silent man, talking neither to his employers nor to his fellow workers. While he continued to visit Lucy with regularity, a storm of rumor gathered about their heads. The taciturn Tom could have dispelled these rumors had he known about them, which he apparently did not. Such rumor held that Tom and Lucy had done away with Cal and Pinkey. Perhaps this rumor was fed by another that the two brothers had dynamited their home cabin in Nash County's Griffin Township and had thus slain their own father, the legendary Fiddlin' Sam and an older brother, whose bodies lay in graves in Nash County. Or, some rumor held, Fiddlin' Sam had survived the dynamiting of the cabin. But, these were just to remain gossip to occupy the men at Gupton's Store at Center Crossing, or the women at fall quilting parties. However, other rumors were making the rounds, but were those just rumors? It was reported that Calvin and Thomas Coley were dark-skinned and had curly hair. But, while these reports alleged that the two had some bit of African blood, they were white men. And, while it is not the purpose of these writings to discuss racial purity, it must be disclosed in the record that Lucy Brewer and Pinkey Wilkins did have slave blood to the one-fourth or one-eighth mixture. At least that story was being told. Whether or not Lucy and Pinkey had some non-white blood, they looked much alike; had dark curling hair and a fair complexion that sun-tanned darker in the summer months. They were both endowed with what was called "good looks" back in 1894.

Again, it apparently was fact and not rumor, that the manner in which the two brothers were openly living with the two women had caused them to leave Nash County for fear of prosecution. That none of the four were natives of Franklin County proved a point of great pride to the then editor of the *Franklin Times* in Louisburg.

It is also apparent that when the four left for their final destination in Norfolk, where they would eventually be located, was not known to the Gold Mine folks. Good riddance had been done. That was the judgment of their neighbors. The leaving of the four saved the Gold Mine people the task of doing what the Griffin Township folks had done; express their "moving" sentiments. Even after the return of Tom and Lucy to the township in September 1892, there were a number of people who were still in favor of giving these two an invitation to move on. But, not being the meddlesome type, the Gold Mine folks left the two alone. Besides who should bell the cat? And, it was true that Tom was seen far less often calling at Lucy's house than had been the case in the past.

Winter came, then spring and again summer and it was recalled that neither Cal nor Tom had been seen in the township for some months. It now appears that Cal and Pinkey were living together in Norfolk. Meanwhile, Tom had met and married a woman whose last name appears only as "King." To this marriage a child was born, the records say, but with name and sex unknown. It could be expected that Tom would not be a faithful husband and the erstwhile Miss King, since he was again seen going to Lucy's house on Christmas Eve, 1893. This was the same day that Lit Western and Irving King went turkey hunting, seeking bounty for their Yule tables.

It is not known whether the turkey hunters got their turkeys, but one of the two did spot a grinning skull under the frost-stripped vines in a ravine not far from Lucy's home. The skull, with the plainly evident hole, was close to a complete skeleton. Dr. J.B. Wheless and Constable "Little Henry" Kearney (distantly related to Sheriff Big Henry Kearney) were summoned to the scene where the skeleton was found. From the condition of the skull, they all agreed that murder had taken place.

Constable Kearney's investigation began at Lucy Brewer's door, just above where the gruesome discovery was made. Kearney voiced to Lucy some of the suspicions that the body was that of Calvin Coley and that Cal had been done away with by his brother Tom recently seen in the neighborhood. Lucy said that this was not so and exhibited a letter from Calvin mailed in Norfolk, The letter was written by Pinkey since the two brothers were illiterate. But, the constable pressed further with his questions, and a few minutes later Lucy broke down and told the story of the slaying of the Jewish peddler. In return for talking, Lucy asked for protection, since a human life apparently meant little to the two brothers and she felt that her own life might be in danger. It was quite possible that Lucy was not too pleased at the news she had received about Tom's wedding to the former Miss King.

Dr. Wheless assembled the skeleton in the back of his buggy and headed for Louisburg. Lucy Brewer had been placed under arrest by Little Henry Kearney, who carried Lucy to the Louisburg jail soon after Dr. Wheless had left. Kearney, along with Sheriff Kearney, returned to Gold Mine and formed a posse at Center Crossing to search for Tom, who had been seen that day in the township. It is possible that Tom had been warned by some of his friends that he was being sought by the "law." It was reported that Tom had taken to the woods near the old Portis Gold Mine. Not only was Constable Kearney fleet-footed, but he could track like an Indian. Tom Coley was in custody some twelve hours after the posse started their sweep of the area where he was last seen.

Little Henry Kearney took Tom in custody on Sunday, December 31, 1893 and arrived in Louisburg that night with Tom in handcuffs. Tom must have been doing some thinking on his own: He spent some money in hiring a lawyer for preliminary hearing. He employed Attorney Wiley M. Person.

The Day the Black Rain Fell

Chapter IV

The warrants for Lucy Brewer, charging accessory to murder, and Tom Coley, charging murder, were prepared by Deputy Norman Stokes soon after Christmas Day, 1893. The next morning after Tom's arrest, Lucy Brewer was brought to the courtroom where Tom was offered his preliminary hearing before Dr. O. L. Ellis, who was also a justice of the peace. Tom waived hearing through Wiley M. Person, his lawyer, and Dr. Ellis ordered him held for the Franklin County Grand Jury without bond. Because Lucy had been placed in jail some days prior to Tom's arrest, she had been given a preliminary hearing before Justice of the Peace J.B. Denton. In this hearing, she entered a plea of "not guilty." Word of mouth spread the news of the tragedy and both Lucy's and Tom's hearing were well attended. Both would be held in jail until the next meeting of the Franklin County Grand Jury in a term of court starting January 22nd, just three weeks after the New Year of 1894. At her hearing, Lucy made a full statement about the murder, and this statement was committed to writing by Magistrate Denton.

Sheriff Kearney had not been idle. Based on information from Lucy, the sheriff wired the Norfolk police to detain Calvin Coley and Pinkey Wilkins. The Norfolk police arrested the two of them there. They were returned to Louisburg by Sheriff Kearney and Deputy Stokes in early January of the New Year. Dr. Ellis gave the two their preliminary hearing before they had been in Louisburg for two hours. Like Tom, Calvin waived hearing and was bound over to the Grand Jury. And, also, like Lucy, Pinkey set about saving her own hide by giving full detail of the slaying. Her story was almost identical to the one that Magistrate Denton had written as related to Lucy. Again, like Lucy, Pinkey pleaded not guilty. If either Pinkey or Calvin were represented by lawyers in their hearings is not known.

The day of the black rain drew nearer.

Chapter V

Mr. S. Stern, president of the Saint Moses Montefiore Congregation in Richmond, came to Louisburg and arranged for the bones of Samuel Tucker to be shipped back to that town so that a traditional burial could take place. There, in Richmond, in consecrated ground, all that remained of the peddler was interred. The burial ground was not too far from the Synagogue where the young man had often worshipped.

In the next few days, Mr. Stern talked with several members of his synagogue and collected funds for the prosecution of the murderers. Stern, accompanied by H.M. Smith, Jr., widely known in legal circles, arrived in Louisburg in mid-January and soon called at the office of Charles M. and P.H. Cooke, a father-son legal combination. The Cookes were thus employed to assist the State of North Carolina in the prosecution of the murderers. The district solicitor would have excellent, and obviously well-paid help, in his efforts to hang the Coley Boys. Stern and Smith later returned for the trial and while the latter sat at counsel table, Stern always had a front row seat at the court proceedings.

The Day the Black Rain Fell

Chapter VI

ohn Grey Bynum, judge of the North Carolina Superior Court, stepped from the Louisburg Railway passenger car on Sunday afternoon, January 21, 1894. He passed a smiling black man who held the reins of a one-horse rental buggy. Because his bag was not too heavy and the day was mild, Judge Bynum felt the walk to his boarding house would do him good. The several other passengers on the train had also decided to walk to their destination. So Judge Bynum, striding along, crossed the single-roadway Tar River bridge just below the railway station.

A reporter for the Raleigh *News and Observer* was in the small group that alighted from the train. His newspaper intended to give the trial full coverage with daily telegraphed reports. The reporter had previously tried to interview Judge Bynum at the Yarborough House in Raleigh. The judge had arrived that afternoon on the East North Carolina Railway from his home in Greensboro. The judge would not talk about a case in which he would probably preside. Besides, he knew nothing of the case except what he had read in the *Greensboro Patriot* about the discovery of the body and the subsequent arrest of the four persons involved in the slaying. It was apparent that the Southern Associated Press was giving wide distribution to the story.

Judge Bynum walked around several muddy spots in the dirt walkway leading up North Main Street. A former captain in General Johnston's last-ditch fight to save the

Confederacy some thirty years before, Bynum carried himself in an erect military manner. He turned to the brick-paved path that led to Mrs. Robert Pernell's house. He was greeted at the door by Mrs. Pernell, a widow for some years whose boarding house was known for good accommodations and excellent food. Having stayed with Mrs. Pernell on two previous occasions, Judge Bynum knew that he would be served a cold Sunday supper but with plenty of fresh-made coffee for himself and the other boarders at the home. The judge had time to refresh himself from the sooty travel on the railway and to toast before a small coal fire in the grate at the hand-carved mantel in his room.

The ringing of a hand bell downstairs called Bynum and the others to their supper at six o'clock. A young minister at the table was asked to say grace after which several covered dishes were opened for supper. A gleaming white coffee pot also arrived from the kitchen and was put to much use during the meal. As the diners were completing their repast, Mrs. Pernell brought in a white coconut cake under a glass bell. The fine cake completed the meal. There had been a small talk over the supper after Judge Bynum had been introduced to the other guests. The judge told of his trip down from Greensboro by way of Raleigh, but it was over the moist cake that one of the boarders broached the subject that was on the minds of each of them.

"I supposed you will get to hear the Coley case?" came from a young minister at the judge's right.

Heads all around the table were raised at this question

and a coffee cup poised in mid-air, on its way to Mrs. Pernell's lips.

Bynum waived the question aside with a speculation, "I probably know far less of the Coley case than each of you." And to Mrs. Pernell, he added, "This is delicious cake."

Although invited to go with a group from the house to evening services at church just up the street, Bynum declined, declaring that he would rest. He then bade the others goodnight and went up the stairway to his room. But the judge could hear the buzz of conversation around the table after he had taken his leave and before he reached the top of the stairs.

Judge Bynum was not being rude in dismissing the minister's question so quickly. He felt that he knew nothing of the facts of the case and was reluctant to discuss with local people a case upon which human lives could depend, as well as, the fact there is always so much misinformation, rumor, speculation and hearsay in a case of such high local interest as to possibly implant prejudice, and he must be scrupulously fair. The judge felt that he could preside at the trial impartially, but he did not want his mind filled with information that was probably inaccurate, biased, and colored with many different personal opinions.

Judge Bynum heard Mrs. Pernell and, probably the young minister and one or two others, as they left from the front of the house. The judge's room faced the street, and he heard and watched a small group of students from the Louisburg Female Academy accompanying their lantern-bearing chaperones to the evening devotions.

Having lighted his green-shaded kerosene lamp, the judge sat down to read the Raleigh newspaper he had produced from his handbag. The lamp was adequate, but he much preferred and sorely missed the Edison electric lamps that he installed in his Greensboro home just the year before. He knew that electricity could be made to do a lot of things. Electric power was all the talk in conversation about the Great Chicago Worlds Fair which would open in May. He also knew first-hand that this electricity could kill having presided at a civil trial involving the wrongful death of a child from a charged trolley cable from a street railway in Greensboro. The jury had assessed three thousand dollars to go to the parents of the child from the street railway company.

The return of the bevy of girls through the street heralded by a few minutes the footsteps and sounds of Mrs. Pernell and her group returning. With his newspaper finished, Judge Bynum banked his fire with ashes, undressed and climbed into the big feather bed. Before sleep came, the judge mused upon how simple the job of being a judge seemed and how complicated it could become in actuality. A judge must be totally absorbed in the evidence given during a trial. Even the phrasing of a sentence in a warrant could possibly mean freedom or imprisonment; life or death for a defendant. Every part of the testimony could be subject to objections by attorneys on the adverse side. An objection would immediately require a ruling from the bench. Because the rules of evidence were both complex and controversial, these rulings in themselves, could mean much to the outcome of a trial. The judge also knew from experience that he was going to face a Bar that fully followed the adversary principle in practice. These young Franklin County lawyers were in the habit of full practice, neither giving nor allowing quarter from the adversary. While this type of vigorous practice was the rule in most of Judge Bynum's courts, there were some jurisdictions where the Bar, composed of elder statesmen attorneys, induced both long and boring court proceedings. Bynum much preferred the Louisburg-type of court where there was aggressive new blood in the bar association. The bright youngsters, their shingles still glitteringly new, were intent on building their own budding reputations by climbing over the legalistic remains of older lawyers. But, these older men, conscious of their own carefully built fame and practice and with the knowledge and experience that comes only with time, were just as intent to see that these youngsters got their comeuppance in a proper manner. Of course, this aggressive type of court was harder on the judge and kept the bench right on its toes. However, the judge believed that aggressive law practice meant a far keener and better system of courtroom practice and resulted in far better and fairer law enforcement.

Most of the seats in the courtroom were taken when Judge Bynum told Sheriff Kearney to open the court session of Monday, January 22, 1894. After the sheriff had completed his traditional court cries, the jury rolls were called and the oath taking of the Grand Jury was finished. Bynum made a brief talk to the eighteen men of the Grand

Jury, explaining their duties. He then proceeded with other court business, accepting pleas of guilty to some of the smaller crimes and misdemeanors on the docket. On Tuesday morning the Grand Jury, as required appeared in court to turn in true bills of indictment for murder against Calvin and Thomas Coley. Judge Bynum approved the court appointment of Wiley M. Person and Frank S. Spruill to defend the two, stated that the trial of the Coley Boys would begin on Thursday morning and ordered Sheriff Kearney to summon a special venire of two hundred men to appear for examination as possible jurors on Thursday.

Solicitor John M. Woodard announced that no indictments would be sought against Lucy Brewer and Pinkey Wilkins. The two women, the court was told, would appear as witnesses for the State against the Coleys. It was suggested that the two should be kept in custody as material witnesses. That afternoon, following a recess, Calvin and Thomas Coley were brought in handcuffs to the court for the formal arraignment. Attorneys Person and Spruill also stood by their clients for this formality.

"And how will you be tried?" the clerk intoned, as the formal pleas of not guilty were entered.

"By God and my country," Person and Spruill answered for the two men.

"May God have mercy on your souls," said the clerk to complete the formal part of the ceremony.

Once again in handcuffs, the two prisoners were hustled back to the jail by the deputy and the jailer.

Judge Bynum reflected upon the task before him. He

felt keenly the underlying unpleasantness of trying men for their lives. He felt once more that burden of sentencing to men to be hanged might be his. While the judge felt strongly about the Bible dictum of an "eye for an eye," he had never hesitated to carry out his duty when called upon to do so. He did have some reservations in reconciling public hangings in this "age of enlightenment and electricity" as the current growth of the United States was now called.

This was 1894. The country was once again making progress while recovering from the grievous scars of the Civil War. President Cleveland had predicted nothing could stop America in a steady growth. The President had stated in his New Year's message that the world was rapidly growing smaller with new, faster steamships and that electricity might eventually light the world. Steam locomotives were now making over forty miles an hour between New York and Chicago. News was spreading by telegraph into print the day after it happened, and there was great potential in the new telephones. The Civil War was not thirty years gone by and remained only a far past, if still bitter, remembrance. The carpetbaggers had been mostly cleared out of the State House in Raleigh and another free election, it was hoped, would soon see corruption finally out of the State government. North Carolina was cleansing itself from the dirty involvement of the war. There was new interest on every hand for what was going on in other parts of the country. There was much public interest in the struggles of promoters to hold a heavyweight prizefight for the world title in Jacksonville, Florida. Gentleman Jim

James J. Corbett was world champion. The contender was Jim Mitchell from England. Boxing was against the law in Florida, but the fight was staged only to see the promoters and the fighters arrested. After the payment of fines, the participants got to keep most of the twenty thousand dollars that fans had paid to see Corbett knock out Mitchell in the third round. One could also learn that fire had destroyed parts of the buildings of the Chicago Worlds Fair, slated to open in May and that the widely known entertainer, Miss Lillian Russell, was soon to wed. A great mansion, (or was it a castle?), was under construction at the Vanderbilt estate near Asheville. The Vanderbilts had even built their own railroad to haul in materials and workmen for the castle and hundreds of workmen at the project were even housed in dormitories near the mansion.

Newspaper readers also wanted to learn about the trial of the Coley Boys, since that trial had interest in the kaleidoscopic play upon the emotions of human beings. All the elements of avid public interest were present in the Coley case.

It was against this background that Judge Bynum approached the courthouse on Thursday morning, January 25, 1894, and through a traffic jam of wagons, buggies and people. The weather was clear and cold. But, by simple method of summoning two hundred special jurors, the word that the trial was about to start had been spread. The judge dourly thought that every one of his two hundred special jurors must have brought several other persons along. Also, it was January; farming was at a standstill and something like this only came along once in a lifetime. The judge understood people wanting to see the trial, but the crowd could cause problems; and this is what happened.

The first problem arose as Judge Bynum was warming his hands before the stove in the clerk of court's office. He had heard the ominous creaking of the support timbers in the courtroom over his head. The judge had scarcely rubbed the chill from his fingers when Sheriff Kearney and several courthouse workers approached him. The courtroom, they reported could possibly collapse. Even now, would-be-spectators were trying to work their way through the throngs at both the front and back stairways to the scene of the trial. The sheriff reported that the press of people had folks even standing and sitting in the large windows of the room. Many of the summoned jurors had not been able to get into the courtroom at all. With the assistance of Kearney and Stokes, the judge worked his way up the rear stairway, into the crowded courtroom and to his bench. Every seat, standing, sitting, crouching against the walls. The place had a foul odor emanating from the areas around the two coal-burning stoves in the room. The crowding had resulted in over-warmed bodies, scorched woolens and baked shoe leather.

The judge called for Kearney to open court. Then his order was clear. The courtroom was to be cleared of every person not necessary to conduct the trial. Bynum informed the spectators that a number of the special venire had been unable to get into the room. Almost an hour was required for the officers to separate the jurors, witnesses and even lawyers from the mob. Finally, at eleven o'clock, Calvin and Thomas Coley were brought into the room and seated with their lawyers, Spruill and Person, at the counsel table. The sheriff had cleared the space around the two stoves, and a chilly blast from one of the open windows had the room smelling a lot better. The selection of jurors was ready to begin.

Bynum glanced at Wiley Person and Frank Spruill, the two lawyers that he had appointed to defend the Coleys. Both were fine lawyers, reputable and capable. Person was the elder of the two and an experienced courtroom strategist. Spruill was well learned in the law in spite of his comparative youth. Yes, the judge thought, the Coleys would have just as good a defense as could be provided. The Coleys were seated now, next to their lawyers, handcuffs off and were conferring with Person and Spruill in whispers.

At a second table within the small enclosure before the bench sat Solicitor John M. Woodard, flanked by H.M. Smith, the Richmond lawyer, and the two Cookes, Charles M. and his son, P.H. Four to two, the judge thought, but he had to admit that it looked as if the prosecution would be ably carried out.

Woodard was a fine solicitor, experienced and clever, a good jury pleader, although somewhat given to bombast. The elder Cooke was waspish, resourceful and a strategist without peer in courtroom action. The younger Cooke had yet to make his mark well known, but he had studied law and practiced under his father's wing. As for Smith, the judge had heard of him only by his reputation as a brilliant trial lawyer and able to command high fees. Smith had gained considerable reputation as a patriot with brilliant appeals to the Supreme Court on some of the carpetbagger legislative acts which were declared unconstitutional. Mr. S. Stern, employer of Smith and the two Cookes, sat in the front of the spectator's section, watching the proceedings through oval pince-nez glasses.

"Is the State and defense ready to start jury selection?" the judge asked.

When both had agreed they were, the judge turned to the clerk and told him to call the first juror.

The day of the black rain drew closer!

The Day the Black Rain Fell

Chapter VII

"With malice and forethought, did kill, murder and slay Samuel Tucker," the warrants read.

Spruill and Person knew that they had a tough one.

Since their appointment by Judge Bynum and Person's brief appearance for Tom Coley at the offered preliminary hearing, the two lawyers had worked hard in their preparation. They had met often to discuss the case and had visited the Coleys in their cells for lengthy interviews for some peg upon which to hang their defense. They had researched the law books in their respective offices, but nowhere in the heavy books had they been able find anything to give much comfort in precedence. The State's case was far too pat. The testimony that Lucy and Pinkey would give would normally constitute an open and shut case. Possible difference could develop between the testimony offered by one sister and that offered by the other.

Even if the lawyers could develop major differences in the evidence offered by each woman, they would be grasping at straws, since the major evidence, they felt sure, would be gruesome and very much alike. At this point, they were not even sure that they would offer the defendants in testimony, since they were fully aware that the prosecution would develop any deficiencies that might have already been in testimony. Once you put a defendant on the witness stand, you had to let the prosecution cross-examine and might even prove the prosecution's case. That is why, in so many criminal trials, the defendant does not take the stand.

The State's two main witnesses remained in custody, but were now seated with the other witnesses near the front of the courtroom. The defense would, quite naturally and as far as the court would permit, attack the credibility and character of the two women. This was to lower their believability in the eyes of the jury. The defense lawyers knew that it very well might harm their case if the slow-witted Tom took the stand. The elder of the two Coleys just did not have the intelligence to make a good witness. And the elder Cooke could probably make hash out of Tom on cross-examination. It appeared that the defense might just take a chance and put Calvin on the stand, but that decision would have to wait until the trial had progressed. Should they put Calvin on the stand, it would be in an effort to prove that the slaying of the peddler had been in the heat of anger, and not premeditated. If they could do this before the jury, and the jury believed it, then the gallows would be cheated. Should Cal take the stand and be convincing enough, then he might save his own life and that of his brother for a life term in prison. So, that must be their plan for the defense. Develop, if possible, from the women's testimony of the slaying, that it had been done in the heat of passion. If that was not practical, then, put Calvin Coley on the stand for that purpose. Both attorneys agreed that this might not be a good plan, but it was the only one that they could come up with from the circumstances surrounding the case. Lucy and Pinkey must be cross-examined in every possible way.

The Day the Black Rain Fell

Their credibility and character as citizens must be attacked at every opportunity.

Person and Spruill were determined that the two women would earn their immunity from prosecution. Both felt that the women should be on trial for having enjoyed the proceeds of the crime. The most damaging part of the evidence to come would, of course, be the whispered conversation had nothing to do with the peddler, it was possible that the money the peddler had been carrying could have excited the curiosity of the two Coleys. Should the jury construe that the conference was the actual plan to kill the peddler, that could possibly knock out their only defense and they were likely to do just that. Other essential elements of the crime to be proven beyond a reasonable doubt was the malice as well as the forethought and the actual slaying itself. Person felt that the State could provide a motive for the killing in the contents of the peddler's pack and the money that he was carrying. Person's legally trained mind shuffled the facts, as he knew them, over and over. Always, he came to the same conclusion. If the jury believed slaying in the heat of anger, it was possible for them to come in with a second degree verdict, saving the life of one, or both of the defendants, but for this to happen, there had to be some break in the case and great deal of good luck.

The senior defense counsel was understandably gloomy when he began examining jurors.

Chapter VIII

nce the courtroom had been partially cleared of the great press of spectators, the two-hundred venire men had places to sit or were standing along a wall. Some of the prospective jurors were too near the stoves for comfort and others were too far away to feel the heat from them. The wide window that had been opened to air the courtroom had now been closed against the January breezes that were blowing outside. The first venireman was called into the jury box.

Charles W. Cooke, later to become a legendary figure as a superior court judge, was given almost unlimited hand by Woodard and Smith in juror selection. This selection process was one of the main reasons that Cooke had been selected as prosecution attorney. Cooke knew the people of Franklin County, their thinking and their beliefs. Of course, Person and Spruill were not novices in this part of the deadly game. They, too, knew the people of Franklin County and how to get the best possible jury for the defense.

The voir dire, as part of the jury selection is called, went on.

Nineteen venire men had been ordered to step aside by either the court, for preconceived opinion, or by the State, or by the defense team when J.T. Hight became the first seated juror. Nine more men were questioned before J.E.T. Ayscue becomes the second juror. The thirty-eighth man examined was L.B. Perry, who became the third juror. The sixty-first examination produced Levin Phillips, as juror number four. Judge Bynum, becoming aware of a growing hunger, consulted the large gold watch from his pocket and declared a recess until two o'clock. Sheriff Kearney called the recess after the judge had warned those seated jurors to avoid all contact with the witnesses and the public.

Shortly after court reconvened at two o'clock, the sixty-sixth panel member, M.E. Joyner, became the fifth juror. J.H. Upperman, number seventy-four on the list, became the sixth juror. Six more panel members were dismissed for having a pre-formed opinion, but the eightieth examination produced R. F. Brantley as the seventh juror. J.H. Conyers, subject of the eighty-ninth examination, was the eighth juror seated. Then some fifty men met with disapproval before Joel H. Harris became juror number nine. H. R. Richards became juror number ten. The one hundred eighty-first examination produced B. M. Alford as the eleventh man. With only ten persons left in the special venire, Woodrow Barton filled the last seat in the jury box. Following the empanelling of the jury, Judge Bynum felt that since it was four o'clock, there was scarcely time to get into the evidence. He gave the jury very strict instructions not to discuss the case and avoid all outside contacts. A bailiff was appointed to take charge of the jury, see that they were fed and taken to their accommodations that Sheriff Kearney had arranged for them at a local hotel. The judge told the jurors that the bailiff could serve as their outside messenger in getting word to their families of their service. The recess was called by Sheriff Kearney until 9:30

The Day the Black Rain Fell

Friday morning.

A light drizzle was falling when court opened on Friday, January 26th. This time, Sheriff Kearney and Deputy Stokes stationed themselves at the courtroom doors to see that only the principals of the trial and sufficient spectators to fill the empty seats were admitted. Hundreds more were refused admission, since the judge had told Sheriff Kearney to avoid all standees, if possible. Those that were turned away by the sheriff were with regret since the sheriff was, after all, a politician and he was concerned as to what a courtroom refusal might do to his political future. The judge had been emphatic in instructing that the trial be conducted in an orderly manner, which was just not possible with all two hundred venire men and other spectators standing about the room, as had been the case on Thursday morning.

With opening ceremonies done, Solicitor Woodard set about proving that a murder had occurred. He used Dr. O.L. Ellis to prove that the bones he had examined, along with Dr. Wheless of Center Crossing, obviously belonged to a small man, who had met death from the blows of some heavy instrument to the skull. Sending the peddler to the house where he met death was told about by N.C. Gupton, who had no room for the peddler. Woodard and Cooke also introduced evidence of finding the bones near Lucy Brewer's house.

"Lucy Brewer, take the stand," came from Woodard.

A glare about the courtroom quieted the murmur that ran through the spectators, as the judge pounded his gavel. Lucy was sworn on the tattered Bible on the bench and followed with giving her name so softly that the judge had to remind her to "speak up."

Lucy raised her head and faced the jury.

Again came, "My name is Lucy Brewer."

This time her voice could be heard in the far corners of the courtroom.

"Mrs. Brewer," said Mr. Woodard, "Would you please tell the court and this jury just what happened at your house on the evening that Samuel Tucker met his death?"

Carefully and in a strong high voice, Lucy related the story that she had told the Gold Mine folks and the magistrate. Spruill and Person listened carefully, making notes on paper before them for points upon which to cross-examine. Both of the defense lawyers sat forward in their chairs as the woman related the whispered conference between the defendants on the night of the slaying. Person noticed that Solicitor Woodard was referring to some papers in his hand. These papers were probably the confession that Magistrate Denton had put into writing from Lucy's story.

This, then, was the key. This whispered conference between the two men now seated at their side, Person knew might possibly prove malice and premeditation. This was the one thing that would, or would not put his clients on the gallows trap. If the jury believed that this conference between the two defendants had been an inception of a plan to kill, then the case was surely lost. In any event, Person knew that the woman's testimony had been damaging to even his small hope of a second-degree verdict. Woodard went on to clarify some statements that Lucy had made and then turned to the defense table and said, "Your witness."

Where Spruill and Person had spent little time as the solicitor introduced the circumstances of the case to the jury, now they were fully prepared to tear down the testimony and the character of Lucy Brewer.

As was his custom, Person began his cross-examination with deliberate slowness. His voice was soft, almost gentle. There was a half smile on his face. Carefully he probed Lucy's testimony to bring out minor details of her evidence. Scarcely noticed by the jury at first, Person's voice was growing stronger and stronger; his questions more searching; and his manner more belligerent. Now he faced the jury and boomed out at the witness at his back for a minor clarification of a point in her evidence. Then, he turned to Lucy with a finger shaking toward her and in a voice low and almost menacing, he asked, " Are you Tom Coley's mistress?"

There was no immediate answer from the witness stand.

"You know what I mean by the question, don't you? It means did you sleep with Tom Coley like you were his wife? Did you live with . . ."

Both Woodard and the senior Cooke were on their feet with objections about badgering the witness and giving the witness enough time to answer.

"Overruled. Could be relevant to the matter under inquiry," came from the judge.

The judge instructed the witness, "Answer the question."

The woman's head lowered again. "I was." she answered.

Once Lucy had made her initial admission, she seemed to realize that the even further admissions could do no greater harm to her reputation than that which had been done already. She noticed that Tom was watching her with a frown of puzzlement on his face, as if he did not realize what was happening, but the defendant's case had suffered damage. When Lucy confessed her involvement with Tom, she had ruined her character with the jury, but she immeasurably increased her believability with that group. She had become a highly credible witness.

Bynum overruled several objections from Woodard, as Person had brought out several other supposedly moral lapses in the witness's past, including the flight from Nash County's Griffin Township, at the invitation of the law.

In the end, Lucy's reputation lay soiled and tarnished before the court and the jury, but the jury was watching her intently. She had told the truth about her past. Had she told the truth about that whispered talk between Tom and Cal Coley?

Person and Spruill realized at once that the stratagem of attacking the character of Lucy Brewer had backfired. They had been counting on Lucy trying to defend her character, which they had been prepared to tear down and possibly expose her as telling untruths on the witness chair. The defense lawyers realized that the jury now believed everything that Lucy had said. Since the woman had not chosen to lie about her past, then most likely she did not lie about the events at her home in Gold Mine on the night of the murder. The two defense lawyers, almost silently agreed that they would be forced to put Calvin Coley on the stand.

H.M. Smith, Jr. realized that he had been watching an expert, if unsuccessful, cross-examination. Although Person had shredded Lucy's character before the jury in efforts to impeach her testimony, he had failed in damaging her credibility. To the experienced Richmond lawyer, it appeared the State's case had been immeasurably strengthened. After all, Lucy Brewer was not on trial. Smith looked at Person and then felt a bit sorry for the defense lawyer, but such things were calculated risks that any lawyer took when he cross-examined. These things could boomerang and this one certainly had. "Wily" Wiley Person had failed in the first part of the plan to save the lives of Tom and Calvin Coley.

Person sat slumped in his chair, his face a grim mask, as Woodard clarified a few points on Lucy's testimony on re-direct examination. Woodard again tendered the witness to the defense and sat down. Spruill and Person conferred in whispers and then, from Person came, "No questions."

Lucy, her head held high, left the witness stand as another chorus of whispers came from the spectators. All eyes followed her as she made her way to a seat in the front row of the audience beside her sister, Pinkey Wilkins. Although Tom Coley's eyes followed her every move, not once did she look directly at her lover. Tom took his eyes from following Lucy as Charles M. Cooke arose and called out, "Pinkey Wilkins, take the stand."

Charles Cooke's first question came as a surprise to the defense lawyers.

"How long," Cooke asked Pinkey, "has it been since you have seen or even talked to your sister, Lucy Brewer?"

"Over a year," the witness answered.

Cooke then brought out on direct examination that the two sisters had been held in separate jail cells, on separate floors, of the Louisburg jail since Pinkey's return from Norfolk and that prior to that, they had not see each other in over a year. Therefore, it was apparent to the jury that not only could the sisters not communicate with each other, they had had no chance to relate their story to each other or to rehearse the story of the slaying. Person looked at Spruill, as the younger attorney shrugged his shoulders. From Pinkey, the lawyer elicited that fact that Sheriff Kearney must have kept them apart for the very reason that was now being made clear to the jury, so there could have been no collusion in preparing the same story to tell. From Pinkey, it was introduced that she had arrived in Louisburg in early January and had been placed in a second floor cell, while Lucy had remained on the lower floor of the jail.

Cooke pressed on with his examination and the tale that Pinkey told was identical to that earlier related by her sister. Another knot was tied in the hangman's rope by this revelation. The jury got the point; so did the defense lawyers, who conferred again in whispers. Spruill arose and made a perfunctory examination of Pinkey. Obviously Pinkey was just as intelligent as her sister and just as obviously, Spruill was not going to make the mistake of attacking Pinkey's character. P.H. Cooke asked to recall N.C. Gupton to the stand. Again, Gupton clarified his story of sending the young Jew to Lucy Brewer's house and of his warning to the peddler of the poor reputation of the house.

Spruill got to his feet when Woodard announced that the State had rested its case. He called the names of J.W. Ervin, J.B. Denton, E.J. Lanier and Arrarah Jones. Each of the witnesses testified that the two Coleys had good reputations for keeping the peace. A fifth character witness was disqualified from testifying due to a legal technicality. When Spruill had finished with the first character witness, he tendered the witness to the State for cross-examination. The four men at the prosecution table looked from one to the other as each of them continued making notes while shrugging their shoulders in complete indifference. Each of the four prosecutors busied themselves with papers while one of them answered, "No questions."

This little tableau was repeated when the second character witness was offered for cross-examination. What the court was witnessing was a ploy used often in jury trials. The defense witnesses were just being ignored; in a strong message to the jury that these witnesses are not worth our time and they certainly are not worth your time. This, of course, was part of the courtroom strategy.

Person, sitting on the edge of his chair when Spruill offered the first witness to the State, now appeared ready to spring to his feet, highly incensed at the indifference of his opponents. Person was also getting red in the face, for he recognized a ploy that he, himself, had used in the past to good effect. By this casual denial of their right to cross-examine these witnesses and the making of such an elaborate show of indifference, the prosecution was deliberately downgrading the witness in the eyes of the jury.

Spruill examined the third character witness, then tendered him to the prosecution. For the third time, there was the elaborate shoulder shrugging and the feigned indifference from the prosecution table. Again, the "no questions" came from one of the four. Person's neck was growing redder above his starched white collar. Spruill was cracking his knuckles when he finished with the fourth character witness.

"Your witness," he stated to the prosecution.

Charles M. Cooke arose to his feet, to nail the little drama home.

"Your honor," he said, "I thought we had clearly indicated that the State has no questions to even dignify these so-called witnesses to the alleged characters, if such things exist, of these two defendants."

Person exploded out of his chair.

"Your Honor," he shouted, "I object most strenuously to this attempt by the prosecution to argue the jury at an improper time." Person was spluttering now. "It is unethical—prejudicial to these defendants—designed to unduly influence the jury—cheap vaudeville performance."

The defense lawyer sat down, glaring at Cooke, who

stood, smiling benignly to the jury.

Cooke and Spruill, who was now on his feet, began speaking at the same time to the judge. After much shuffling of papers on his desk, the judge found his gavel and pounded for order. The lawyers took their seats under the glare of the bench. The judge's order "be seated" was delivered to attorneys who were already in their chairs.

Judge Bynum then upheld Person's objection to the brief speech by Cooke. Then the judge turned to the jury and instructed them to disregard the remarks made by the prosecution and the defense in previous outbursts. He then turned toward the counsel table and lectured the adversaries on courtroom manners and legal ethics. Then the judge cleared his throat and announced a ten-minute recess. "Shades of Edwin Booth," he thought, as he left the bench.

The ten-minute recess, like all courtroom ten-minute recesses, lasted twenty minutes. The recess did find the defense lawyers in deep conference. The result of that conference was that the defense had to offer Calvin Coley to testify and thus play the only card they had left.

When Judge Bynum called the court back to order, the name of Calvin Coley was called by Person. The young defendant took the stand and his oath. Now was the time for the defense to prove no premeditation, if they could do so.

Person's first question got Cal Coley's name and his age. After giving his name, Cal stated that he was twenty-three years of age.

"How old is your brother, Thomas Coley?" came from Person.

"About twenty-seven," Cal replied, twisting his hands together, with his brow beaded with perspiration.

Although Calvin Coley was illiterate, he was far from a fool. He knew, as many in the courtroom knew, that his life and the life of his brother might depend upon what he had to say and how he said it. Cal also knew that he was not doing too well so far. He was trembling at the life and death importance of what he was about to tell. Cal tried to tense his hands over the witness box railing, but even this failed to stop the trembling that had come into his hands. How he needed a drink. Person was standing beside Cal now, as the witness wiped his forehead with his sleeve. The lawyer spoke softly, even gently, attempting to instill confidence in the frightened witness.

Person spoke, "Tell us, in your own way, just what happened on the night of June 30, 1892?"

The lawyer remained at Cal Coley's side.

"Well, this is the only thing we have to offer," he thought to himself. He felt just what Cal was undergoing and the young man was doing much poorer than he had imagined. Even now, Cal was looking at the judge then towards those twelve people who held his life in their hands. Person noticed the witness when he gripped the edge of the witness box, but the witness's hands did not stop trembling. The jury also saw those white-knuckled, trembling hands. Perhaps the obvious strain that the younger Coley was under might elicit some sympathy from the jury: that, were these the hands of a man who plotted with his brother to take a human life? If doubt still remained about that question, Cal Coley was apparently now ready to dissolve those doubts. The defendant gained some control over himself and began speaking from a throat that was dry and aching.

"I had been visiting Pinkey Wilkins for about four months," Cal realized his voice was pitched too high for his tightened throat. He lowered his voice and continued. "I never saw Tucker but twice in my life, the night of the fight and another time at Mr. Taylor's in Nash County. I was courting Betty Nelms, but the peddler told her that I was a kinky-haired nigger and she discarded me."

"I was at Pink Wilkins house when the peddler came there. He asked her if he could spend the night and she told him 'Yes.' Tom came in a short while after. We ate supper and the Jew went to lay down. After awhile, he went out and took a seat in the passage. Tom and I went out soon afterward. I asked if he wasn't the man who called me a kinky-headed nigger. He disputed me twice and rose to make fight. We went together and struggled for about five minutes. Then Tom held him and I reached around and go an axe with which I struck him twice. The women were standing at the door and a window at about this time. There was a light in the kitchen nearby. The women had been on the bed just before the scuffling started."

Cal realized that his words, which he had had to rehearse in case he might have to testify, were now running together. He paused, looked at the jury, all of whom were now sitting forward in their chairs, moistened his lips and continued.

"I felt that the peddler had died in our scuffle. So, Tom, my brother, and I took the peddler into the woods. The women went with us. When we came back, I kicked over a bundle in the yard and found that it contained money. The women took the money and counted it. We divided up the goods and the next day we went to Durham and the day after we went to Norfolk."

The four prosecutors had been making notes during Cal's brief recital. The four conferred briefly while Person took Cal over some of his testimony. Of course, Person tried to emphasize the self-defense that just might have arisen in the evidence. Person also brought out Cal's anger at the peddler—that there was no premeditation there. Cal knew nothing of any whispered conference between himself and his brother prior to the fight. This, then, was the lawyer's only hope. A killing in the heat of anger and not with malice and forethought. That, and outside chance from this evidence, might render a second-degree verdict.

Woodard got to his feet for the cross-examination. His first question was designed to shake the witness even further. It did that very thing to the witness, already shaking from telling of that night.

"Has your brother, Tom, got a normal mind?" came from Woodard.

The witness bristled visibly. "He's got just as much sense as I have," Cal stated, defending his brother's mentality.

Person and Spruill again conferred in whispers. Woodard had anticipated one of their defense strategies. Seated in the spectators section were two men, who could be called as witnesses, ready to testify that Tom Coley had far less than the average amount of "sense." They would also testify that Calvin Coley did the major decision-making for the two brothers when they were together. The two defense lawyers again had their heads together as to whether to not elicit some change in Cal's flat statement about Tom's intelligence. They took a few brief minutes to decide against such a move, since to do so would further jeopardize Cal's believability before the jury and they would be in a position of impeaching their own witness. Both lawyers also realized that what little chance they had previously had of saving the life of the elder brother was blown away by the witness's statement.

Woodard bored in. With question after question, the solicitor shattered what little character that Cal Coley had in the eyes of the jury. Carefully, Woodard enlarged the holes that he and the other prosecution lawyers had noted in Cal's evidence. The solicitor worked at length on the differences of the witness' story and the identical stories given by Lucy and Pinkey.

"Would you mind telling us again how you," Woodard said, as he turned and faced the jury, "stumbled, I believe you said, over the package of money in the big yard in the dark of night?"

Woodard could see Person fuming and expected an objection, but the defense lawyer had no ready basis for an objection, and apparently did not wish to call further attention to Woodard's obvious inferences.

The solicitor turned again to Cal, before the question

could be answered, and asked, "You took the Bible in your hand and promised to tell the truth, didn't you?"

"Yes, yes, I did," came from the witness.

"Well, then, what were you and your brother whispering about after supper on the night you two murdered the peddler?"

"Objection," exclaimed Person. "Invading the province of the jury—making conclusions and argument in the examination of a witness."

The objection drew a "sustained" from the bench. The judge then warned Woodard about making conclusions in examination. The judge then turned towards the jury and instructed them to disregard any conclusions that they might draw from the solicitor's question.

"Apply your own minds to only the answers of the witness," the judge further instructed.

Woodard nodded to the bench, then rephrased his question.

"What were you and your brother whispering about after supper on the night that the unfortunate peddler got murdered?"

This time Spruill got to his feet protesting to the bench, "He is doing the same thing again, Your Honor."

Tiredly, Bynum once more instructed the jury to disregard any inferences from the question and then instructed the clerk to strike from the record the solicitor's question.

The judge then turned and glared toward Woodard, as if preparing to speak. Woodard was faster and proposed that the witness answer the question.

"What were you and your brother whispering about that night after supper?" He avoided a lecture from the bench. The solicitor smiled at Judge Bynum, who settled back in his chair. The smile was then turned on the jury, apparently in contrast to the black looks coming from the defense.

Woodard thought, "Yes, gentlemen of the jury, disregard the inferences of the question. Forget what I said, forget what I said, if you can."

Cal Coley was grateful for the brief respite from his questioner. He hadn't the faintest idea of what the angry exchange between his lawyers, the prosecutor and the court had meant, although he felt that the exchange was not in his favor. Now that he had had time to consider his answer to the question, the witness spoke, "I don't remember whispering to Tom after supper."

Woodard stated, "You heard Lucy and Pinkey tell about you whispering with Tom, didn't you?"

"Yes, I heard them tell about it, but I don't remember it."

The solicitor was not content that Cal would have the last word and said, "You have a very convenient memory, don't you?"

From that, Person and Spruill shot to their feet.

"I will withdraw the question," quickly came from Woodard before the defense. Cal had said that he had killed in the heat of passion. If he had convinced the jury or established a reasonable doubt, then he might possibly have saved his life.

Woodard walked to the counsel table, then turned, "Your honor, I have just a couple more questions for the witness."

"Go ahead," came from the bench.

"Mr. Coley, this Jewish peddler—he was a large man?"

"Oh, no," replied Cal. "Kinda a sawed-off short man, weighing about one hundred and thirty pounds."

"How much do you weigh?" came from Woodard.

"About a hundred and sixty," came from the witness.

"Your brother Tom is about the same size that you are? Is that right?"

"Yes," came from Cal.

Person and Spruill frowned at each other. They, along with the jury, could immediately see one small man in mortal combat with two muscular men, each weighing one hundred and sixty pounds. A quite uneven match!

As the jury got that picture in their minds, Cal was suddenly aware that he had put his own case in a very bad light.

"No further questions at this time," Woodard told the court.

Woodard had been effective in cross-examination. The solicitor had brought out the seeming oddity of Cal stumbling over the moneybag in the dark. He had stressed how Tom had held the slight peddler, while Cal had struck the fatal blows. There were few, if any, unanswered questions in the minds of the jurymen.

Oddly enough, Woodard felt compassion for Spruill and Person. Not many years ago, he had been a defense lawyer for a practically indefensible murder case. You did what you could, then left it up to twelve good men and true; a jury of your peers.

A friend of Coleys, whose name could not be heard in the spectator's section, was called to the stand by the defense. This witness stated that Tom Coley's mentality was not fully normal. This, of course, attacked Cal's believability, since he had stated that his brother had just as much sense as he did. The question about Tom met with immediate objections from the prosecution and was sustained from the bench. Grounds for this objection were that it was the province of the jury to determine if Tom had enough mentality to carry out the crime he was charged with. An exception was made to the ruling. The calling of this witness showed that the defense was in dire straits and had decided to attack part of the evidence of their own witness. This was a last minute decision by the defense in a desperate effort to possibly save the life of the elder brother. Then, the defense rested.

In rebuttal testimony, Woodard offered David Leonard, who corroborated Lucy Brewer in statements that she had made in the Gold Mine community about the slaying. These statements, which had been brought out earlier by Lucy, fully agreed with what the woman had told that day in court, Leonard testified.

Woodard then called Aaron Dietz, also a Jewish peddler, who testified that he was well acquainted with Tucker and that Tucker was a small man of about one hundred and thirty pounds.

The evidence was concluded at four o'clock, at which time there was a recess.

As court reconvened, P.H. Cooke, the junior of the prosecution counsel, made the first jury pleading. He dealt quietly with the evidence and asked the jury to do their duty according to the law and their oath.

Wiley Person was next to address the panel. He did not go into great detail on the testimony but directed his considerable oratorical talent to an impassioned speech of pleading for the lives of the Coley brothers. He quoted liberally from the Bible on forgiveness and compassion. He pleaded for a second-degree verdict and gave as his basis, "certain uncertainties," in the evidence.

Person thought, as he seated himself, how he had followed an old legal maxim: If you have a strong case, plead the evidence; a weak case, plead the Bible. Person hoped that the members of the jury had never heard of the old saying.

Charles M. Cooke was next before the jury. He began immediately to praise the people of Franklin County.

"Our people," he said, "Deserve praise for the way in which they have not taken the law in their own hands at the commission of such a foul crime. While this crime is an atrocious one," he said, "I'm glad these unfortunate murderers have been allowed a fair trial, and an impartial trial, before a jury of their own countrymen.

Cooke continued in what the *Franklin Times* called a "very feeling manner" and reminded the jurymen of their high obligation to the great name of the people of Franklin County.

The lawyer concluded with "I feel that you members of the jury will do, without hesitation, what the law requires of you to do."

Frank Spruill was required to wait until after the supper recess to make his pleading to the jury.

Meanwhile, Deputy Stokes had lighted the oil lamps about the courtroom, including the green-shaded one on the judge's desk and those on the counsel tables. Judge Bynum had heard that Louisburg had contracted for a steam-driven electricity generator, but that work had not been completed.

Spruill was glad of the recess. As a comparative newcomer to the bar, he felt that following Charles M. Cooke before the jury was somewhat like following Lincoln at Gettysburg. Spruill also hoped that the supper recess might allow the jury to forget some of Cooke's clever pleadings.

When court reconvened at seven o'clock, Spruill made an important step in a long and distinguished career that later led to the position of division counsel for the Atlantic Coastline Railway.

Even Charles Cooke, a past master of the art of jury pleading, marveled at the way that Spruill pitched into his plea. Piece by piece, Spruill took the evidence apart to hold each part before the jury in the light of his logic. The speaker's voice fell and rose as if some master's hand controlling his emotions and rhythmic cadence of his words. Time and time again, he drove home bits of favorable evidence with fist pounding into the palm of his hand. He played the reasonable doubt theme until even the weary jurors sat forward in their chairs. Made hoarse by his ringing words, Spruill completed his speech almost in a whisper. He thanked the jury, turned wearily to his chair and sat down.

The reporter for the *Franklin Times* commented in print that "Spruill made one of the best speeches ever heard in the courthouse." And, even in 1894, that was a broad statement, since Charles Cooke was famous for his jury pleadings. Person was highly skilled in the art. Young Will H. Yarbrough, who had studied law with Cooke, was also making a name for himself as a courtroom speaker, after having begun practice in 1891.

Person and Spruill had approached Judge Bynum during the course of the trial and asked under what law their clients would be tried.

By means of explanation, the two lawyers had found it necessary to explain how the 1893 legislature had changed the murder laws and designated "first degree, second degree and manslaughter and limited the punishment for each category. Since the trial was taking place in 1894, a different homicide law was in effect. In light of earlier laws, persons found guilty of homicide were sentenced to hanging. The two attorneys had petitioned the court to instruct the jury under the new law in effect at the discovery of the crime. Person and Spruill had entertained even their faint hope of a second-degree verdict for one or both of their clients, thus saving one life, possibly two. But this particular move had been a gambit for the defense—they knew that and Judge Bynum knew that. They all knew that the crime had occurred in 1892 and was normally to be tried under the law then in effect.

Of course, the defense lawyers had failed in their petition to Judge Bynum on the matter of the law, and it is quite possible that they expected to fail. But, in failing, they did have another point upon which to base their appeal to the Supreme Court if the verdict went against their hopes. It later did develop that this point was offered to the North Carolina Supreme Court in its obligatory review of the Coley case.

When Frank S. Spruill had completed his widely acclaimed speech to the jury, Solicitor Woodard made his pleading. The solicitor was brief, holding the floor only twenty-five minutes in a summation of the evidence and a reminder to the jury of their duty.

Smith, the Virginia lawyer, did not address the jury. His principal duty at the trial seemed to be acting as liaison with S. Stern, his employer, and the other attorneys for the prosecution. Besides that principal duty, there was nothing that Smith could add to what had been done by the two Cookes and Woodard, plus the fact, that a Harvard accented First Family of Virginia talking to an already weary jury might even antagonize them.

Referring often to books of law and notes on his desk, Judge Bynum charged the jury for fifty-eight minutes. During the charge, the judge moved his green-shaded lamp to the left so that he could face the jury and still have the benefit of the yellow light on his papers at the same time. During his charge, Bynum said, "If you believed the testimony of Calvin Coley, then both defendants are guilty of murder."

Person and Spruill winced.

The judge continued, "It has been brought to my attention that these defendants should be tried under an act of the legislature passed last year which designated homicide in degrees and fixes the punishment thereof. But, I charge you now, gentlemen of the jury, that these defendants are being tried under the law that existed when this offense took place."

Then, the judge gave his interpretation of the law then in effect.

The judge completed his charge at ten o'clock p.m. on that Friday, January 26th, 1894. As the jurors filed into their chairs at the conference room, the judge ordered the court to be "at ease."

But, being at ease was far from anyone's mind. Tom and Cal Coley sat erect in their chairs at the counsel table. Obviously, ill at ease. The lawyers talked together in low tones or conferred briefly with the judge. The crowd in the courtroom slowly diminished in number. The spectators had presumed, and as it developed, correctly, that the verdict would not be quickly given.

At eleven o'clock, the judge instructed the bailiff to lock the jury up for the night in their quarters. He then brought the jury out and instructed them in not discussing the case among themselves or with any other person until they were back in their jury room the next morning. Court recessed until nine thirty Saturday morning.

Chapter IX

A bright January sun was streaming through the windows of the courtroom when Judge Bynum ordered Sheriff Kearney to open court. The jury was returned to their conference room to work further on their verdict. The judge settled himself behind his desk and opened a Raleigh newspaper that had just come in on the nine thirty train. The Raleigh reporter had telegraphed in his front-page story at about four o'clock the previous afternoon, before the jury pleadings had begun.

Judge Bynum looked over the courtroom, beginning to fill with spectators. Only Woodard and Wiley Person were in place at their tables. Charles M. Cooke and his son came in about ten o'clock and talked with Person. They told the defense lawyers that he had seen Attorney Smith and Mr. S. Stern off to Richmond on the morning train to Franklinton, where they would change for the Richmond train. Cooke said that he had instructions to wire the verdict to Smith.

Calvin and Thomas Coley were left in their cells by orders of Judge Bynum. The defendants' two women friends were absent from their places in the front row of the spectator's section. Again, the courtroom was almost filled.

But, at this time, the spectators had guessed wrong. The jury was not yet ready.

At twelve thirty, following another consultation with his gold watch, Judge Bynum ordered the jury to be brought into the courtroom.

"What is the nature of your disagreement, a matter of law or a matter of fact?"

"A matter of fact," the foreman replied.

"In that case, I cannot help you. You must rely upon the evidence that you have heard," the judge replied.

Person and Spruill, now in the courtroom, noted the conversation of the judge with the jury in the absence of the defendants and noted another exception to use on appeal. A weak point, even though the defendants might have been in their seats when even a small part of their trial was taking place.

Court had been reconvened for almost an hour after the noon recess, when Tom and Cal were brought in handcuffs through the rear door of the courtroom. With their handcuffs removed, the two sat tense and sweating in the overheated room.

Judge Bynum sat with lawyers in an anteroom and talked of the Civil War and how the practice of law had changed in this rapidly changing world.

Back on the bench at five thirty, the judge again consulted his watch and ordered the bailiff to bring the jury into the box. Once more he inquired as to the nature of their failure to agree. This time the foreman told the judge that their failure to agree was due to the interpretation of one of the judge's instructions. Bynum repeated the questioned instructions, then he said, "I have given you the law. Your oaths require you to return a verdict in accordance with that law as I have laid it down for you, and if you are satisfied beyond a reasonable doubt that the defendants, or either of them, are guilty of murder, you should return that verdict.

When the jury had returned to their conference room, Person filed an exception on two points. First, that the first inquiry of the jury should have been in the presence of the defendants. Second, that what was said to the jury in regards to their oath in returning a verdict of murder, by the court, was grounds for exception. When the exceptions had been entered, the judge once more brought the jury in to instruct them on their conduct during the supper hour and a recess was then declared until seven o'clock.

Court reconvened and by eight o'clock Judge Bynum was seriously considering withdrawing a juror and declaring a mistrial. The twelve men had been considering in their minds the evidence some twenty-two hours. But, as long as there was a chance that a verdict might emerge from the jury room, they would stay in session.

Bynum felt that the jury was not in agreement due to the fact that a verdict of guilty would mean the hanging of one, or both, of the defendants. How often he had encountered this inborn reluctance of men to punish their fellow men, particularly when the punishment was death. This sentiment must have been running strong in the jury room. It might take some time for the majority of the jurors—if such a majority existed—to get the minority around to their way of thinking, whatever that way was. The judge again consulted his watch, ignoring, as he often had, the courtroom clock, which had come to disagree with his watch by several minutes during the week.

"I shall wait another hour," Judge Bynum informed the

courtroom.

The jury, like the gradually dwindling crowd of spectators, wanted to be on their way home. Farm chores needed doing. Firewood must be brought in. Sunday services at their churches were just ahead.

Only the ticking of the courtroom clock interrupted the stillness of the room. Several of the spectators were visibly nodding. Muffled voices could be heard from the jury room. The big kerosene lamps flickered visibly and added to the dark circles over them on the ceiling.

The courtroom clock showed nine, when the jury room door opened. Tired and disheveled after their three days on the case, the twelve took their place in the jury box.

"Have you agreed on a verdict?" the judge asked the foreman.

"We have, Your Honor," came from the foreman.

"The defendants will rise," ordered Bynum.

Cal and Tom, along with their lawyers, rose and faced the jury. Close behind the two men stood Sheriff Kearney and Little Henry Kearney. Movement had ceased in the courtroom except for the busy ticking of the clock. Cal Coley clenched his fists until the hard nails bit into his palms.

First to move was the clerk, who paced the creaking floor to stand by the jury. The clerk read the formal charge against Calvin Coley, then asked the jury "How do you find the defendant, guilty or not guilty?'

"Guilty, as charged," came the foreman.

Calvin Coley would hang.

"So, say you all?" the clerk asked.

All members of the jury nodded their heads.

Immediately, the clerk read the formal charge against Thomas Coley and again the answer came, "Guilty, as charged."

"So, say you all?" came from the clerk and all twelve heads of the jury nodded.

Thomas Coley would hang.

Calvin Coley's face went chalk white. He looked in anguish towards the judge, then at the jury. Thomas Coley looked dully about the courtroom, apparently unable to comprehend what had happened. The two men seemed hardly aware when the handcuffs were again placed about their wrists, nor did they even seem aware when Judge Bynum set Thursday, February 1st, as the date for sentencing.

The courtroom came alive as the judge thanked the jury for their services and gave them a verbal discharge. Since the time was growing late, it is understandable that some of the jurors failed to prove their attendance at the clerk's office and pick up vouchers for the few dollars due them for their service. Some of the jurors have not been paid, to this day, for their service on the Coley trial.

On February 1, as court opened, Cal Coley, then Tom, received orders to stand before the bench for judgment.

Judge Bynum did not get to read immediately from the paper in his hands, as Frank Spruill arose with a motion to set the verdict aside and grant a new trial. Spruill argued his motion for several minutes, upon the five different exceptions that he and Person had drawn up for the presentation to the Supreme Court. These exceptions were as follows: (1) the witness to Tom Coley's mental capacity should have been allowed to testify in full; (2) the law on homicide in effect at the time of the slaying was, in effect, not applicable to the Coley case since a new law had been enacted before the discovery of the crime; (3) that the judge made prejudicial error in instructing the jury that the holding by one defendant of the victim was not consistent with the legal conception of slaying in the heat of passion; (4) a witness to the character of the two defendants should have been allowed to testify, although a technicality existed that he had not properly qualified himself to answer a question; and (5) the two defendants were not in the courtroom when the jury was first asked about their disagreement.

Cal and Tom had remained standing while Spruill argued his motions and stated the five points to the judge. When Judge Bynum denied all the motions, Spruill accepted in order to complete the necessary legal work for the required appeal to the Supreme Court.

The two defense lawyers then stood beside their clients. Once more Judge Bynum picked up the paper upon which he had written his judgment. The judge looked at Tom and Cal before his voice was heard in the far reaches of the courtroom. All motion had stopped in the room as the judge read:

"It is adjudged by this court that the prisoners at the

bar, Calvin Coley and Thomas Coley, having been found guilty of the charges against them, be remanded to the custody of the Sheriff of Franklin County and safely kept until the second day of March 1894, on which day between the hours of ten o'clock in the forenoon and four o'clock in the afternoon, will take the said Calvin and Thomas Coley to the place provided by the Commissioners of Franklin County for the execution of criminals and there hang them by the neck until each of them is dead."

The judge then bowed his head and said, "May God have mercy on your souls."

The formal motion of appeal was then filed as the two condemned men shakily returned to their seats. Almost immediately, the officers told the men to rise and the two men were led from the courtroom to their cells.

Chapter X

But what of Lucy Brewer and Pinkey Wilkins?

Assumption must now take over where the written records end. So, we must assume that the two women, once they had completed their sordid roles in the trial of the Coleys, left Franklin County. Their leaving was likely at the request of the authorities. But, whether they returned to Nash County, from whence they and the Coleys had come, is not known. However it is known that a number of the Gold Mine folks were hostile to the two women. Not that they approved of the Coleys going unpunished, but many felt that the two women should not have been given their freedom after their admitted complicity in the crime and their enjoyment of the proceeds. In any event, their disappearance from the records indicates that the leaving of Lucy and Pinkey must have been soon and permanent.

Author's Note: The names of Lucy Brewer and Pinkey Wilkins are used here as a matter of convenience since those names appeared most often in the records. It has been impossible to find their actual family name. The record of the North Carolina Supreme Court states that their names were Lucy and Pinky (notice the dropped "e"), a system that most records do not follow. Most records indicate that Pinkey's family name was "Williams." In all the confusion of the old records, it is apparent that they were sisters. Establishing the fact that they were married, had been married, or were married at the time, or were ever marred, common or civil law, defies the researcher. So, it must be left that the family name of the sisters was either Wilkins, Williams, Brewer or Brower—take your pick. Records in existence indicate that one of those names might be the correct family name for the two women who played a sordid part in the murder and the trial of the Coley Boys.

Chapter XI

om and Cal Coley were healthy eaters, generally active and muscular, with heights around six feet. Tom was slightly taller of the two and with weights set forth before, of about one hundred and sixty pounds when they first entered the Louisburg jail. The inactivity of confinement and Sheriff Kearney's substantial food had caused them to gain weight. Thus, they had fattened while their case wound through the Supreme Court. They were, in effect, fattened out of condition to engage in a footrace for freedom, which is exactly what happened. Had they remained fit, the outcome of their bid to escape might have been different.

But, being overweight, it developed, made it a mistake for the two condemned men to plot with one John Perry, a black man, and also an inmate of the Louisburg jail, to engage in a jailbreak on a Monday some weeks after the Coleys were convicted; however, plot they did.

Perry was well muscled, lean and in good condition for running. He proved that later. Perry apparently was not a good citizen since the charges against him included larceny and a charge for a previous jailbreak. The key to the jailbreak plans of the Coleys and Perry was the Reverend W.B. Morton, a Louisburg Baptist minister.

Morton had visited the Coleys regularly since their appeal to the Supreme Court had extended their execution date. With great patience, the minister had been teaching the Bible to the two men and was seeking their conversion to Christianity. It was Morton who had comforted the two men when they learned of their next execution date as Friday, July 13, 1894.

The Coleys knew that Morton would visit them on that particular Monday morning, just eighteen days from the execution date. They knew that because the minister had said that he would be there. He was on time, arriving at the jail about ten o'clock. Prior to the minister's arrival, the Coleys and Perry managed to get into an empty cell in their block. Perry had secured a piece of oak wood from the jail's fuel supply. Cal had managed to break off a leg of an iron stove and had attached this weapon to his wrist with a string. When Jailer Pinnell opened the big barred door of the cellblock to admit Morton, the three escapees rushed out, swinging their weapons. Pinnell was apparently unhurt in the onslaught, but Morton suffered a long gash in his forehead, when struck by the oaken stick in Perry's hands. The five fell in a tangle of arms and legs all the way down the stairway from the jail's upper floor. The Coleys and Perry, swinging about them with their weapons, untangled themselves from the melee and dashed out into Louisburg's East Nash Street. All three of the escapees headed east, legs pumping in a headlong dash for freedom.

Pinnell got his pistol from his small office and started in hot pursuit while calling to several passersby to stop the fugitives. Right after Pinnell came Reverend Morton, dripping blood from his head wound. Several people joined in the chase. Besides, Pinnell, lean and in good condition, saw that he was overtaking the Coleys, who had chosen to run side by side, and whose excess weight was beginning to tell on them. Some four hundred feet from the jail, Pinnell, still out-distancing the Coleys, aimed his gun and called for the two to stop. Seeing their flight was futile and looking at the jailer's aimed gun, the two Coleys stopped and held up their hands. Morton, now holding a white handkerchief to his wound came up. The minister, along with two others who had joined the chase, followed Pinnel who, at gunpoint, escorted the Coleys back to their cells.

The Coley Boys had taken their last breath of freedom; a freedom that lasted almost fifteen minuets. The jailbreak try had once more aroused the citizenry; hundreds came to look at the jail and to discuss, over and over, the attempted break of the Coleys. There was much said as to what might have happened if the two had separated in their run from the jail.

As the Coleys came to a halt under Pinnell's gun, they were in front of Wilder's Foundry on East Nash Street and as they surrendered, John Perry, open shirt flying in the wind of his superlative speed, was disappearing into the woods near where Nash Street now intersects with Bickett Boulevard.

Why didn't the Coleys take separate routes in the run for freedom? The old comment came back, that Tom did not think on his own; that Cal was still doing the thinking for the two and Tom was going to be right at the younger brother's side.

Sheriff Kearney, out of breath from running, arrived as the two men were being put back under lock and key. The sheriff mounted the jail steps and announced to the several persons who collected that a twenty-five dollar reward would be paid to the person or persons who brought in the fleet-footed John Perry. Several people joined the sheriff in search for the fugitive, but all the searchers returned empty-handed by nightfall.

Early the next morning, Daniel Debnam was starting his chores at the Knib Thomas farm in Sandy Creek Township, when he heard snores from the second floor hayrack in the barn. Although Debnam had not heard about the escape, he did arm himself and awakened his employer. The exhausted John Perry was prodded from the hay in the loft by a shotgun in the hand of Debnam. The farmers tied Perry's hands with plow line and got him into the farm wagon. Before the farmers set off for Louisburg, as a precaution, they tied Perry's feet. Some two hours later, they delivered Perry to the Louisburg jail. Sheriff Kearney paid the captors their twenty-five dollar reward, then prepared the warrant for Perry for the latest jailbreak and the assault on Reverend Morton.

The Day the Black Rain Fell

Chapter XII

Captain S.S. Meadows and his blue-coated Franklin Guard went on duty at the jail the day of the escape. Ostensibly, the guard was there to prevent another escape by the two condemned men, but there were other reasons for their presence. For some time, Sheriff Kearney had heard persistent rumors that some of the drinking pals of the two prisoners would attempt a jail delivery for the Coleys. Kearney knew that the two men did have a number of friends in Gold Mine and in nearby Nash County, who felt that the court deal too harshly with the Coleys. Meetings of Coley sympathizers did occur, rumor has reported, for some organization to free the two men, however, apparently there was enough sober thought at the meetings to understand the futility and risk of such a bold venture. It is also possible that the presence of Captain Meadows and his guardsmen, on round-the-clock duty, discouraged any foolhardy plans that might have been brewed. In any event, if plans were made to deliver Cal and Tom from the Louisburg jail, they were never carried out.

And the day of the black rain drew nearer.

The Day the Black Rain Fell

Chapter XIII

A t the side of the jail, the heavy timbers of the double gallows were in place. The structure was open on three sides and a canvas was placed over the covering framework for protection from the sun. There was space for eight chairs behind the swinging traps for the official witnesses.

Calvin and Tom remained in good spirits, the Reverend Morton reported, even though they could hear the hammering in the construction of their gallows. It is possible that their good spirits were caused by rumors that they had heard of their prospective delivery from the jail. The gallows were now completed except for the placing of the two ropes. Sheriff Kearney had one rope already prepared. The second rope would arrive with a visiting sheriff.

Friday, July 13th arrived, hot and humid and the day began without clouds in the sky. Sheriff Kearney was at the jail soon after dawn, to make sure that his jail would not be breached by the Coleys or their friends. In addition to the guardsmen, the sheriff had sworn in several deputies of the day for crowd control and security. By nine o'clock the town was rapidly filling with people. All roads into town were thronged with people and all were thick with the dust, fine as good flour, was already hanging over the Tar River valley. The air grew more humid as the sun rose higher in the sky, now beginning to pile high in the west with thunderheads. Nash Street slowly filled with people, who stirred up more dust, making it difficult to even breathe. By eleven o'clock, an estimated ten thousand people, according to one local reporter, were in the town to attend the hanging. Even the Louisburg train had its passenger car loaded with filled seats and standees. The sweating people pressed closer and closer to the solid cordon of guards and deputies about the gallows. Some of these spectators saw Sheriff Kearney test the gallows traps with sandbags. Each of the two traps worked perfectly once the sherrif merely kicked out the supports.

Among those who had alighted from the train and in the throng crossing the Tar River bridge, was Sheriff W.M. Page of Wake County, who carried a large brown paper package under his arm. Page had brought Calvin Coley's rope. Sheriff Kearney already had Tom Coley's rope in the jail. Now, this was no ordinary rope that the Wake County sheriff had brought. This rope had a history—a gruesome history.

The rope that Page brought had been used by the then Sheriff J.R. Nowell, first on August 4, 1883, for the hanging of Henry Jones for the murder of Deputy Sheriff Alvis H. Blake. On January 10, 1890, the rope had been used by Wake Sheriff J. Rowan Rogers to hang J.C. Parrish for rape. In 1891, Sheriff J.L. Currie of Moore County had borrowed the now famous rope to hang William Bostick for the murder of Jerome Currie. Sheriff John W. Cooke of Guilford County next borrowed the rope to hang Charles Blackburn for murder and Charles Reynolds for murder. As Sheriff Page carried the storied rope, he remembered that it had been promised to Sheriff Hamilton in Alamance County, to hang Bob Madkin for rape, which was scheduled for August 10, 1894. But, first Sheriff Page had his own use for the rope, to hang Orange Page for the murder of Rosa Haywood in Wake County, this being slated for August 4, 1894.

Sheriff Page finally made his way to the jail and was greeted and with a handshake by Sheriff Kearney. Together, the two sheriffs went to the gallows and with the help of a long ladder, put their two ropes in place. Sheriff Kearney again tested the traps and measured the distance of fall with the two ropes. If all went well, and that is not a good word for hanging, the two men would fall exactly six and a half feet when the traps were opened. A shorter fall could break a man's neck, but it was considered best to have this much fall. Thus, the neck was broken and the victim died painlessly. Of course, this would prevail if the noose remained under the ear of the condemned man. But, if the rope should slip to either the front or the back of the neck, then that "unclean" hanging would result.

Earlier, Cal and Tom had eaten a good breakfast. Although it was not reported, it is assumed that the two men were allowed to order their favorite foods. At least, that was the custom.

After breakfast, the two men had shaved and dressed themselves in the two suits provided by the sheriff. Following that, Kearney had completed the task of reading the death warrants to the two men, but the sheriff went even further. As he had done several times in the past, he asked the two men about the rumored slaying of their brother and the attempts on their father's life. And, as steadfastly as they had done in the past, they denied any part in their brother's death or in the dynamiting of their father's cabin in Nash County.

Reverend Morton and the Reverend B.R. Pernell, a Missionary Baptist minister, had been with Cal and Tom since ten o'clock. Morton still bore a livid scar on his forehead from the jailbreak encounter with John Perry, some eighteen days before.

In the west, the early bright blue skies had long since been obscured by the massing towers and battlements of cumulus nimbus clouds, steadily growing darker. The crowds of spectators were edging closer and closer to the jail fence with each person trying to locate a position in front of the scaffold. Dust rose in the humid air over the town as the bridge and street clattered with even more arrivals for the event in our Roman arena.

Noontime came and what the Raleigh *News and Observer* called a "perfect swarm of humans" elbowed their way into choice positions near the jail yard. The crowds grew so dense that several of the Franklin Guards had to help clear the way for the official witnesses to get to the gallows and mount the stairs to the platform and the empty chairs. When the witnesses were in their place, the sheriff began forming a "death march" procession at the jail entrance. At twelve thirty the Franklin Guards and the deputies of the day began forming two lines for an aisle from the jail door to the gallows steps. The crowds pushed closer to watch the procession as thunder muttered and lightning flashed in the West. In the procession were Dr. E. E. Malone and Dr. E. S. Foster. The preachers, Morton and Pernell, followed the doctors. The two ministers were followed by Tom Coley, with a deputy on each arm. Then came Cal, also with a deputy on each arm. The marchers climbed the steps to the gallows platform, while the deputies kept close guard on their prisoners. Soon the deputies were adjusting the ropes about the Coleys' necks. Some hangings have used black masks for the faces of the condemned, but they were not offered here. Now the crowd grew silent as the thick dust continued to rise on the vagrant breezes from the approaching storm.

There was a slight flurry in the crowds and the guards and deputies began clearing the path for two men driving a wagon which approached the gallows. On the wagon were two pine coffins.

Cal Coley had raised his eyes as he started up the gallows steps. He flushed and then grew deathly pale. He was visibly shaking as he first saw the ropes. Tom did not even look up, but kept his eyes cast to the ground and the steps. Reverend Morton was the first to speak. His voice cracking with emotion, he told how the illiterate men had been taught about the Bible. He said that neither of the two had ever been in a church or a Sunday school. The minister spoke up, his remarks interrupted by loud crashes of thunder from the approaching storm. He told those who could hear him that Tom had been the first to accept Christ and that later Cal had acknowledged himself as a sinner and had prayed for salvation not too many days ago. Tom had been reluctant to repent, but had done so and accepted Christ as his saviour just three days before the aborted jailbreak. Here the minister fingered the livid scar on his forehead before continuing. Each man, he said, had expressed hope of being pardoned in Heaven for their grievous sins against God and man. The minister closed with a prayer for the souls of the two men. Then, with head bowed, he descended from the platform.

Sheriff Kearney then mounted the platform and asked each man if he had anything to say. Cal turned his head to the sheriff as the noose slowly slipped on his neck and said, "Since the trial, I have been told that if we could have a new trial, it would have been murder in the second degree." Apparently realizing the futility of his remarks, Cal faced the front of the trap, as the rope slipped to the back of his neck.

"I have nothing to say," said Tom.

The sheriff descended the steps and took his place between the two trap supports. Perhaps he should have checked the positioning of the rope about Cal Coley's neck. Cal turned to Tom and said something in a voice that could not be heard by the witnesses on the platform. But, when they again faced forward, Tom was seen to answer something not heard on the platform. Then Cal shook his head, further dislodging the rope about his neck. Apparently Cal was still doing the thinking for the brothers, even as their lives were about to end.

But, what had been asked by one brother of the other?

Did they want to confess to the slaying of an elder brother? Did they want to confess to the dynamiting of their father's cabin? Perhaps there was some dark and unknown crime they needed to expose. Was one brother seeking some kind of assurance? We shall never know. The deputies removed the cuffs from the prisoners and tied their hand with rope and then tied their feet.

It is possible that Cal's noose became dislodged when he talked to the sheriff or to his brother. But, apparently the noose was now behind Cal's neck when the sheriff sprung the trap, or maybe it was the well-polished rope that Sheriff Page of Wake County had brought with him that slipped on Cal's neck.

Outside the gallows, the crowd hushed, waiting tense and expectant. Their silence was broken by the close rumble of thunder as the storm drew nearer. The sun was completely hidden and the dark clouds thickened. The two horses hitched to the coffin-bearing wagon nickered nervously and caused their driver to tighten the reins for fear the animals might bolt into the crowd. A stronger breeze stirred the pall of grey dust that hung over the town and began blowing the dust high in the sky. Sheriff Kearney looked at his watch; it was one fifteen o'clock. Then he quickly kicked out the two supports for the traps. At the same instant that the traps dropped, there was a great flash of lightning and roars of thunder from the storm.

Tom Coley died instantly from a broken neck. His hanging was clean. Calvin Coley was denied that quick death. The highly used rope had become dislodged on his neck and his body writhed and twisted as he slowly strangled to death. One of the doctors began examining Tom, but his examination was largely unseen by the spectators who saw Cal twist in his horrible death throes. The audience, many of whom had their mouths open as if trying to help Cal breathe, watched with frowns as the body of Cal slowed its obscene dance and grew still. One of the doctors began examining Cal and declared him dead several minutes after the other doctor had said that Tom was dead.

Out in front of the scaffold, another doctor, O.L. Ellis, had his head buried in a camera cloth in back of a tripod camera. Tom's body was swaying slightly so, Dr. Ellis had one of the guardsmen hold Tom's leg for a time exposure. That photograph exists today, although quite dim with age.

The records indicate that the doctors worked slowly on the bodies. Their official time for death showed that Tom Coley died at 1:26 o'clock. Cal was declared dead seven minutes later.

The two pine boxes were brought from the wagon, filled with the bodies and placed on the wagon as the first heavy drops came from the skies. Sheriff Page reclaimed his storied rope and hurried through the raindrops toward the Louisburg railroad station. Cal Coley died some seven minutes after his brother, he was the last person to die by legal execution in Franklin County. One other man was later sentenced to be hanged, but he cheated the gallows by taking his own life in his jail cell with the help of a knotted bed sheet.

The black rain that legend always insisted fell on the day the Coley Boys were hanged apparently was due to the large amount of dust raised by the hooves, wheels and feet of an estimated ten thousand persons in Louisburg that day. Your author would estimate from the records possibly three thousand or less than that, but still a large crowd. The dust that these spectators had created was swept high into the sky as the wagon and its two-coffin burden left Louisburg for Nash County. The first rain that fell bore this dust back to earth in large raindrops that even stained the weatherboarding on houses and caused many washes, left on the line, to be redone. This has been borne out by witnesses to the event. It was the privilege of your author some years ago to have interviewed eyewitnesses to the hanging. In particular, one man was a member of the Franklin Guard on duty that day at the Franklin County jail, who gave a concise report of that day, including the black rain.

The black rain soiled everything that it touched, even the clothing of those leaving the hangings. It has been said that the Weather Bureau has mentioned that dirty rain could fall following a dust storm and that is apparently what happened on July 13, 1894.

The wagon bearing the two pine boxes arrived in Wood, in eastern Franklin County late that day. The trip had been bumpy over the unimproved road and the two coffins had slowly worked their way to the rear of the wagon. At Wood, the wagon hit a now muddy chuckhole and Calvin Coley's coffin became unbalanced and fell crashing to the road. The flimsy pine box split open and Cal's body rolled in the mud. The two men on the wagon first shifted Tom's coffin to the front of the wagon so that it would not meet the fate of its twin, then lifted the stiffening remains of Cal Coley to the wagon bed. They looked into the face of the man who had died by strangulation. The eyes of the corpse were distended, and both the men on the wagon turned away from their look with their stomachs churning. They beheld the dead face locked in an expression of unparalleled hurt and fear as if Calvin, being slow to die, had peered briefly into where he was going and recoiled in horror from what he saw there.

The funeral of the Coley Boys took place the next day in Nash County. They were laid to rest next to their brother, who had himself died at the hands of a murderer. There was comment at the time that one of the coffins looked as if it had been split and hurriedly repaired.

Chapter XIV

here were a number of other legal county seat hangings in North Carolina before the Legislature acted to put all executions at the Central Prison in Raleigh. We must remember that the State was growing vigorously with the new technology in science and mechanics. Several people were already producing horseless carriages. A telephone had been placed in the White House in 1887 and such instruments were soon to become commonplace. In just nine more years, the Wright Brothers would make a powered flight at Kitty Hawk.

Throughout North Carolina, more and more people were becoming concerned with the Roman Circus that was being made of the county seat hangings. In 1895, the Legislature made some changes in the law but the county seat hangings continued for the "salutary" effect on the citizenry, but criminals were still committing rapes and murders. The Devil would continue to recruit his subjects regardless of any law.

In 1909 the General Assembly took the step to authorize the installation of the electric chair at Central Prison in Raleigh. In March of 1910, the chair was ready and on the eighteenth day of that month, took its first victim. The county seat hangings were ended.

It is believed that Sheriff Kearney favored the end of the county seat spectacles. It is also believed that John Woodard, John Grey Bynum, Charles M. Cooke, P.H.

Cooke, Wiley Person and Frank Spruill favored an end to the county seat circuses.

Samuel Tucker, the peddler slain by the Coley Boys, knew the history of his people and how they suffered persecution and death over the centuries, but even with that knowledge, it is believed that the peddler, had he been alive to do so, would have favored an end to the holidays that our people were making of the executions.

So it could be argued that the execution of the Coley Boys perhaps served some obscure purpose in helping to bring to an end to the circus that was being made of the executions. This was on the day that the black rain fell in Franklin County.

It was said at a later date, that a lone woman, whom many did not know, stepped forward and tossed a flower in Tom Coley's grave. The woman stepped back after this act, got into a buggy and left the funeral site. The woman had a child in her arms as she disappeared from history and all written records.

Afterward

In search of the story about the legendary black rain that fell in Louisburg, North Carolina, on July 13, 1894, one had to research old newspaper files—where they existed—and talk to a number of persons whose recollections could be used. Some of these recollections were actual, including the mother of Judge Hamilton Hobgood, who was an apparent eyewitness to the flight of the Coley Boys from the Louisburg jail. We shall learn more of this escape later. Again, some of the recollections of Franklin County people were but hearsay, but remarkably accurate in that the Black Rain always entered the story.

Our search began in 1962 and has more or less continued until this writing of this final manuscript in late 1983. There has developed in me a fascination for the people that were involved in the murder of the Jewish peddler in July of 1892, and the final act of the drama in July of 1894. This later date was when the Black Rain came. But, it became apparent that even with using all of the resources available to "flesh out" the story there must still be some "fiction." This was necessary and this name has no real bearing on the story. The attorneys, the judge, the jurors and the defendants are real people. Many of these real people are related to, or ancestors of, a number of present day Franklin County folks.

I wish to express my sincere thanks to a number of Franklin County people who assisted in compiling both the factual and legendary background for this book. Thanks must also go to those librarians who graciously assisted in locating microfilm and other records so necessary to reconstructing the Coley case.

A very special thanks must go to T.H. and Ginger Pearce who have encouraged the final rewriting of this manuscript and who have immeasurably contributed their great knowledge of what you read here. To Judge Hamilton Hobgood, judge of North Carolina Superior Court, thanks for his encouragement and relating some of his own knowledge obtained from his mother, who was an actual witness to the Coley Boys jailbreak. Thanks also to Mr. Charles Dunn of Raleigh, who assisted in making suggestions and corrections to this manuscript. Those errors which do creep into the final edition are not to be blamed on him. Thanks, a great deal of thanks, to the late Mortimer Pleasants, a member of the Franklin Guard—a corporal, I believe—who gave me his good recollection of the happenings on the day the Black Rain fell.

Some of the situations in this book have been interpreted and fictionalized in order to bring out certain facts. But the basic facts are true as recorded in records for those years just before the turn of the century. Those records, insofar as possible, have been verified from those writings that do exist.

—*W. F. Shelton*
1984

The Hanging of Two Brothers
By Miss Mattie Dozier

In eighteen hundred and ninety four
On the thirteenth day of July;
Two brothers—Tom and Calvin Coley,
Were doomed that day to die.

They took the life of a poor Jew,
Who had stopped to spend the night with them.
They took his money and his life,
And all that belonged to him.

They fled from this country for their lives,
And traveled by iron rail.
But woe unto them, they were found out,
And placed in Louisburg jail.

Six months they have lain in Louisburg jail,
Close in their prison cells,
To pay the penalty of their crime.
Which doomed their souls to hell.

And little did they seem to think
That the time was drawing nigh,
When they would be taken from this world,
And not be prepared to die.

Our faithful minister often went,
And plead with them to pray,
That their last hours in prayer be spent
Before their execution day.

And they were cheerful all the time
And seemed to bear it well;
Because they thought that they had friends,
Who would take them from the prison cell.

But, alas! That awful day drew near,
And the bright sun had arisen;
Brave men in their uniforms of blue,
Had kept them safe in prison.

The last week of their lives were spent,
In hearing the hammer and plane,
Building a gallows to take them from their friends,
Whom they would never see again.

The awful day shown bright and clear,
And a great crown gathered;
To see two brothers on the scaffold,
Hang high up in the air.

The hour had arrived, the time had come,
The sheriff and all went in;
No one could tell how they did feel,
When the death warrant was read to them.

Around the lowly jail they marched,
And faced the scaffold high;
And with a strong and steady step,
They walked up there to die.

They did not seem to realize their fate,
Until the scaffold they ascended;
They called for mercy, but it was too late,
For their life on earth had ended.

I knew their punishment was great
But, oh! It was an awful sin,
And that poor Jew's life was just as sweet,
As their lives were to them.

Poor Tom, he was not very bright,
As every one was saying,
But for his brother he done the deed
And died on the scaffold praying.

I hope our Heavenly Father heard their prayer,
As they called for mercy from above,
And save them in the hour of death,
And took them to his throne to love.

I hope that all will think of their fate,
And what a death they died,
And never break the laws of men,
But walk daily by their Saviour's side.

This poem was published in the *Franklin Times* about August 1894. It is used by permission of that newspaper. The author of the poem is believed to have been a Franklin County schoolteacher.

An Uncommon Man

William Floyd Shelton

Storyteller, Husband, Photographer, Father, Mayor,
Brother, Pilot, Theater Operator, Friend, Municipal Judge
Artist, Writer

The Day the Black Rain Fell

Our *"Renaissance" Dad*

Stella Shelton

I'm still not sure how he did it, but "Wimpy" Shelton made quality time for his children, even as he worked three jobs and served as a volunteer firefighter. Story-time with Dad was not standard storybook fare—no, he invented his own unique stories, illustrated them with pen and paper, and of course, the central heroine was yours truly. Not many children can claim to have defeated an "octacat," much less having actually seen one. But I can.

In the real world, Dad brought his kids along on many of his adventures, from trips to the airport to vacations in

Louisburg Theater at night. Photo by the late W.F. Shelton.

the big cities of the nation to fighting fires in the middle of the night. Even with a young family and all those other things, Dad was a passionate consumer of the written word, whether fact of fiction. He subscribed to two newspapers, several magazines, and was never without a paperback book by his chair. The creativity didn't stop at the written word: At varying times in his life, he dabbled in oil painting, pen and ink illustration, sign painting, photography, and music.

Dad was tender, playful, and mischievous. While those qualities are endearing, they can also be crazy-making. My mother's life was never a dull one, and she bore his eccentricities well, though not always silently.

Wimpy and Anne Shelton on their NY City honeymoon.

Louisburg Baptist Church Directory Family portrait; clockwise from top—Bill, Stella, Anne, Wimpy.

Dad's most fun job was his work as manager of the local theater. Even though that meant he had to work evenings, we were allowed to see movies for free. The house sound system was pretty darn good, as I recall, especially when my brother put on his *In-A-Gadda-Da-Vida* album and turned the volume up to 10. My Dad felt the floor shake and ended the nonsense pretty quickly.

When a heart attack nearly killed him, Dad cut back on his work schedule, concentrating his time on his accounting business. How did such a right brain person succeed at such a left-brain job? For Dad, it wasn't about the columns of figures and the Tax Code, it was all about the lives of the people who brought their work to him.

Dad knew a good story when he heard it, so it's no surprise to anyone who knew him that Dad was so fascinated by Franklin County's local history that he researched and wrote a first manuscript of *The Day the Black Rain Fell*. The work went unedited and unpublished for decades. Thankfully, with the urging and help of friends, Dad saw the fascinating story published, just five years before his death.

I am my father's daughter; witness the broad shoulders, weak blue eyes, and fair skin, sense of humor, and voracious curiosity. But despite all of those genetic hand-me-downs—or perhaps because of them—I catch myself reading the world as he would have. I know he would have been thrilled at the reincarnation of *The Day the Black Rain Fell*. Thanks to Wanda Mukherjee for recognizing the value of this story, breathing new life into it, and in so doing, reviving the legacy of my father.

"You Can't Beat a Man at His Own Game"

by Bill Shelton

"What do you win, if you win an argument with a half wit?" my father, William Shelton used to ask me.

I wonder if that was why Dad was so drawn to the story of Cal and Tom Coley's hanging. Tom was almost surely a half-wit drawn into a crime by a cunning and callous younger brother. Did he spend most of his adult life writing it and re-writing it to simply tell the story or was his objective to set right a wrong he thought might have been done to a simpleton like Tom Coley?

Wimpy and the Aeronca Champion airplane he co-owned with a friend.

A rainy Nash Street in Louisburg; Point-of-View, standing in front of Louisburg Theatre, looking toward Main Street. Photo by the late W.F. Shelton.

The new publisher convinced us to add this addendum to *The Day the Black Rain Fell* to honor Dad who had pursued this story and the writing of this book with the same spirited enthusiasm as he did everything in his life.

I learned some lifelong lessons from my Dad—William Shelton, a man who lived his life to the fullest rarely idle, always working and sometimes playing. He was an extraordinary man in every sense of the word. He saw the world in a different context than most men of his time— he pursued flying, art, writing while at one point holding down three jobs.

When I was ten, the Franklin County Fair underway, Dad carried us to the midway with its twinkling lights and bountiful games of chance just waiting for young chaps like myself to lose our nickels and dimes. Never missing an opportunity to teach a lesson, Dad whipped out a twenty dollar bill—now that's the equivalent of $200 in today's dollars. I watched in amazement as we went from one game to the next promptly and predictably losing all our money.

Did Dad lament the loss of that hard-earned $20 bill. Not one bit. In his mind, the money was well spent. The lesson learned: you can't beat a man at his own game and I never forgot it.

My earliest recollections of Dad center around trips to the Franklin County airport to talk with his old flying buddies. Having been in the Civil Air Patrol in World War II, Dad loved to fly. Before I was born he spent as much time as he could in the air that is when he wasn't working. Yet, at heart he was a family man. Shortly after my birth in 1949, he and Mom decided it was time to buy a house. So he sold his beloved plane.

Dad was a classic workaholic, before that term became fashionable. Lots of husbands and fathers during that time worked long hours. In my Dad's case, he was the manager of the Louisburg theater at nights and weekends and a Recorder's court judge during the week days. Recorder's court was the 1960's era equivalent of today's District Court. No law degree was required, you only needed to be elected—my dad's personality and easy going demeanor helped him win the coveted position. Perhaps it was during his stint at Recorder's Court when he became interested in that dark Friday the 13th back in 1894 when a circus of folks came out to see two men hang.

Of course, as a kid I was more interested in his night job at the theater. I saw all the cowboy and war movies for free and back then 15 cents got you a cold drink and candy bar.

Dad went into an accounting partnership with a friend. In 1963, it happened—a heart attack so bad that Mom wasn't allowed to tell Dad that President Kennedy had been shot and killed in Texas. The long and arduous hours spent working three jobs, his lack of exercise, diabetes and smoking caught up with him. On "doctor's orders" Dad gave up the Recorder's court judge job and eventually the theater manager job. He took up golf, lost weight from

Wimpy and Anne Shelton on a cruise.

250 lbs to about 175 lbs and switched from cigarettes to a pipe.

Some of my fondest memories are when Dad and I played golf—although both of us struggled with the finer points of the game. The accounting practice flourished so he bought out his partner. Finally, he only had one job, but old work habits die hard—that is he simply transferred his tendencies to work too much into his accounting business. Dad followed the doctor' advice of napping during the day, weekdays were not different than weekends. Dad got up and went to work.

As we grew older, Stella and I discovered lots of "toys" down at the office, such as an eight-band radio to listen to pilots' conversations, a rock polisher and lots of magic devices to perform for kids who came to the office. Of course, the toys didn't get much use during income tax filing season. Best of all, once the hustle and backbreaking tax season ended, the entire family went on vacation, usually to the National Association of Accountants conventions. My sister and I got to see Boston, Miami Beach and Las Vegas and met lots of accountants' kids.

When I graduated from college in 1971, my Dad offered me a chance to work in his firm for $100 a week. That was a generous offer from Dad and not bad pay for the early seventies, I had no desire for the crushing hours. From my point of view, I saw nearly all of Dad's accountant friends with similar health problems. While I admired Dad's work ethic, I longed to have the time and the good health (eventually) to coach my son's little

Louisburg Baptist Church Directory—Wimpy and Anne Shelton.

league and basketball teams. So instead of joining Dad's firm, I enlisted in the Army Reserve in 1971. I wish my Dad and Mom could have been there when I got my final promotion to Lieutenant Colonel in April 2000. I'm sure they would've been proud.

I sincerely hope that he wasn't offended or too disappointed when I decided to work for Dun & Bradstreet, then the State Revenue Department instead of Shelton Accounting. The accounting practice was sold to an associate and today still bears his name. Dad was diagnosed with colon cancer in March 1989, but worked up until July, as the disease progressed and died of the disease in September, 1989. He never actually retired.

Somewhere during his three jobs, health problems and host of other activities, Dad found the time to write *The Day the Black Rain Fell*. He finished the first draft in the late sixties, but the book wasn't published until the eighties. I was so often asked for a copy—very few exist now—that Stella and I decided to have it re-printed. Our hope is that the book will find an entirely new audience and that the mythology surrounding the Black Rain will continue to be told.

"The Lord must have loved the common man ... because he made so many of them," Dad used to say after observing graffiti or other foolishness around town."

When God created my father he broke the mold. Dad was no common man. I still miss him. Some days, I tell you, I still smell his tobacco pipe.

The Day the Black Rain Fell

Wimpy Shelton; clearly, he made his own clothing choices
for this portrait taken around the time
The Day the Black Rain Fell was first published in 1984.

The Day the Black Rain Fell

About the Author

William Floyd Shelton b. June 12, 1915, Mt. Airy, NC, fourth and youngest child, and only son of Claude A. Shelton and Estella (Stella) Poore Shelton.

The family relocated to Siler City, NC, where he graduated from Jordan Matthews High in 1932. Claude Shelton was the local Gulf Oil distributor, and Stella had a full-time job as homemaker and mother to four.

Bill's sister Frances was a first-grade schoolteacher in Hyde Park, NY. Sister Lucy was a registered nurse in Siler City; and sister Margaret (nicknamed "Mickey") was Town Clerk of Siler City for many years. Theirs was a middle class upbringing with a strong emphasis on education, service, and faith. All four children were blessed with a great sense of humor, so there was much laughter and joy in their household. Stella Shelton passed away in the early sixties from a heart attack. Claude Shelton, maintaining the discipline that governed his life for decades, passed away in the mid seventies, just after his daily walk.

Bill began his postsecondary education at Louisburg College in the early thirties, but the country was still recovering from the Great Depression and money was tight. He was forced to drop out of Louisburg before he earned his Associates Degree. To his credit, Bill was determined to finish his degree. In the mid-fifties, he finally completed all the required credits. Family folklore tells the story of the College Dean John B. York (also a neighbor on Williamson Street in Louisburg) awarding Bill his Associates Degree in the front yard of the Shelton house on Williamson Street.

Most long-time Louisburg residents remember Bill as the affable manager of the Louisburg Theatre. And it may also be said that few actually knew his name was William or "Bill." It seems that Bill's passion for hamburgers earned him the name of "Wimpy," after the Popeye cartoon character.

Wimpy met a local girl—Anne Freeman—and fell in love. The pair were married in a simple ceremony on November 5, 1939. They enjoyed a brief honeymoon in New York City, before Wimpy returned to his responsibilities at the Louisburg Theater.

The couple tried valiantly for a decade to have a child, and there were several very disappointing failed pregnancies. Finally, in 1949, William Claude Shelton was born on March 7.

Shortly after Bill's birth, the Shelton family moved to their new house at 108 Williamson Street in Louisburg.

Four years later, Bill's baby sister came along: Estella Keith Shelton was born on October 14, 1953.

Wimpy's political career had also begun to take off. He served as Mayor of Louisburg in the early 50s and was later elected to a position of Recorder's Court Judge.

With a partner he founded an Accounting business in the early sixties, eventually buying out his partner, naming the business W.F. Shelton, Accountant. To his great delight, a bright employee bought out the business in Wimpy's later years, and the business bears his name today.

Even in his seventies, Wimpy rolled out of bed long

before sunrise, made his own breakfast, and went to the office. Chances are excellent that he did far less accounting work and more of the things he enjoyed. Is there a job title "Accountant Emeritus?" At any rate, he kept his work routine, not only for his own sanity, but for that of his wife, as well.

At 74, he was diagnosed with cancer. His decline was rapid, and mercifully, Wimpy passed away on September 28, 1989, exactly six months after the diagnosis. He is buried in Oakwood Cemetery in Louisburg. His bride, Anne Shelton, passed away on April 3, 1998, from heart failure. They are buried side-by-side in the Freeman family plot.

www.ingramcontent.com/pod-product-compliance
Lightning Source LLC
Chambersburg PA
CBHW032104080426
42733CB00006B/405